JIM OLSON

JIM OLSON
BUILDING · NATURE · ART

INTRODUCTION BY AARON BETSKY

With 550 illustrations

CONTENTS

A PERGOLA
IN THE WOODS

JIM OLSON WEAVES ART, NATURE, AND LIVING TOGETHER

AARON BETSKY

Jim Olson's first project was small and basic. The young man, still learning to be an architect at the University of Washington, set out into the woods with $500 and an idea that he was going to make a place of his own. Olson designed his first shelter in the grounds of his grandparents' weekend house at Longbranch, a community on a peninsula in Puget Sound, with the help of a carpenter. He designed and built by hand a foursquare structure with visible frame and clear proportions—a trim and comfortable shelter, as beautiful as it was humble.

The cabin consisted of a board-and-batten bunkhouse in which the wood created planes that both defined the space and held the building together structurally. Although you can understand the distinct pieces and how they come together, Olson did not intentionally differentiate between them. Nor did he feel a need to establish primary views or a sequence of spaces in this most elemental shelter.

Over the years, Olson has expanded and transformed the cabin four times, and today, it stands as a record of his evolution as an architect. Within the larger structure, he has preserved the original hut, making it a touchstone by which both he and we can measure his progress. Not only is all of his career present here, but from there you can also see the first house he ever designed for a client— the Conry Residence, built in 1966—just across the water.

Today, as in nearly all of Olson's houses, the cabin's main organization occurs along a spine or central axis. This line runs from the main living area in the east to the master bedroom in the west, more or less parallel to the slope. The original cabin sits to the side of that line, marking the transition to a short cross-axis that leads past the kitchen and service areas. On the other side of the axis, the living space opens up to the views over Puget Sound and out to Mount Rainier. The same is true for the other living areas that extend out from the spine, as well as the master bedroom.

While Olson has retained the network of beams and columns that echo the tall firs outside with their branches reaching overhead, both the nature of those elements and the view they frame have changed over the years. Together, building and nature have merged into an experimental array of lumber, plywood, and metal posts and beams employed in various stages of Olson's architecture.

PAGE 8: The beach at Longbranch Cabin. **OPPOSITE, TOP LEFT:** Jim Olson in 1959 at age eighteen building his first cabin at Longbranch, Washington. **OPPOSITE, TOP RIGHT:** Conry Residence, Longbranch, Washington, 1966. Olson's first commission for a residence. View of master bedroom deck. **OPPOSITE, BOTTOM:** View of Conry Residence from the beach.

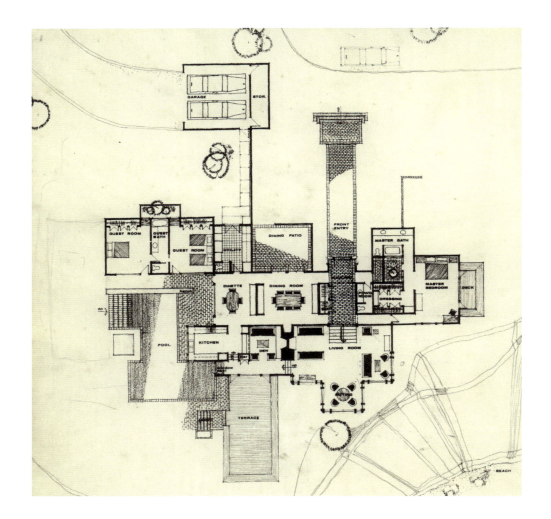

Over time, additions to the Longbranch Cabin grew, becoming more complex and introducing new materials. In the last addition, which Olson completed in 2014, smooth wood surfaces burnished with care by craftspeople stretch between beams that were fitted carefully around windows that seem to dissolve; the sense of peering through the trees while inside the cabin gives the illusion that Olson has invited the forest into the house itself. Today, the interior spaces include a master bedroom, closets, and a bathroom, where once the toilet was a separate structure in the nearby woods.

Sited along the natural ridge of the land, the Longbranch Cabin occupies a space between nature and human territory. Olson's structure asserts that position with a rhythm of connectors, ancillary rooms, and boxes that are, in many ways, the point of the whole construction. A long colonnade reaching all the way from one end of the cabin to the other connects spaces and views both inside and out, from the forest to the water and the mountains.

ABOVE: Floor plan of the Conry Residence. **OPPOSITE:** Mount Rainier seen from Longbranch Cabin.

Olson says he was initially inspired by the architecture of the pergola at Far-A-Way, the area's grand lodge, which he used to visit as a child and that sits adjacent to the Conry Residence. You can see the attraction the structure, which still exists, held for the young man: the pergola is both a container of space and completely open, measured and yet only a fragment. It is possible to feel in place there while still remaining part of nature, which is the whole point of journeying out to the islands and peninsulas of Puget Sound.

The cabin's colonnade is a modern-day version of the central axis that for centuries has been an important architectural device. With its origins in the pathway that connected people to monuments, a means by which humans focused and measured the landscape, the formal axis became a central part of architecture. For centuries, the basic formula for a building consisted of a combination of three elements: the overall layout, defined by geometric proportions; the sequence of principal spaces; and the character, or overall visual appearance and formal nature, of the whole structure.

Though the various ways in which architects responded to the new technologies, scales, and social relations that so radically changed the physical environment starting with the

Industrial Revolution dissipated many of these doctrines—and especially challenged the notion
of the building's character as defined by past forms—the basic armature of these axes and the
apportionment of spaces remained remarkably constant. What tended to happen was that how
you experienced these elements dissolved into abstractions and shifts in geometry or direction,
so that you could only find the order if you looked carefully enough.

The subsequent sense of a loss of clarity and legibility of structure led many architects after
the Second World War to try to find ways in which the sense of clarity the traditional doctrines
had offered—the solidification of centuries of practice and theory—could be regained while using
contemporary materials, working for modern social conditions and scales—and, while responding
to the lack of agreed-upon order, the ephemerality, and the uncertainty that many felt were the
defining characteristics of the modern world, could be accommodated through design. They looked
for new geometries and new ordering devices, while still holding onto some of the old methods
they had learned.

It was in this world that Olson learned to design at the University of Washington, studying
with professors who had been trained in the old academies; these teachers embraced modernism,
and were searching for ways to design in the conditions that confronted them. Prominent among
Northwest architects at the time were Paul Kirk, for whom Olson briefly worked upon graduation,

as well as Ralph Anderson, another mentor
of Olson's. An (almost) native of Seattle,
Kirk had also been educated at the
University of Washington, and practiced in
what had come to be known (after a 1939
exhibition at the Museum of Modern Art
in New York) as the International Style:
flat roofs, simple spaces, as much glass
as possible, and an avoidance of evident
hierarchy. Like many other architects

working in the Pacific Northwest, however, Kirk built his structures not in the glass, steel, and concrete that were most common on the East Coast or in Europe, but in wood, with long overhangs and a slightly rambling composition of pieces meant to fit around the tree and into what were often sloping sites with prominent views.

Olson thus became part of an approach pioneered by architects of the so-called Bay Area School, most notably William Wurster, who explored building with locally sourced materials for a more informal society, while still incorporating moments of order and classical proportions into his work. These architects connected their projects to their surrounding contexts, with building structures hewn from the abundant forest in the region. Their revolution was a gentle one—a way of adapting, abstracting, and making more accessible the grand styles that had once characterized "significant" architecture.

In addition to soaking up such influences, Olson was also profoundly moved by the structures he saw in Europe and North Africa when he traveled there several times after graduating from architecture school. He toured the major architecture sites, but what impressed him most were the ruins in Egypt, in particular Luxor Temple. It was the hypostyle hall there, its thick columns spaced closely together in a field, as well as its long alleys of colonnades, that made him aware of the rhythmic possibilities of such structures. Perhaps it is also significant, given his later love of elongated vertical proportions, that the ruins are overwhelming in their height, especially as the roofs they once supported are missing. The building's bones are what remains, and it is the resonance between these human-made skeletons and the tall conifers of the Pacific Northwest of Olson's youth that is central to the way he developed his architecture.

OPPOSITE: Dafoe Residence, Longbranch, Washington, c. 1960. Residence designed by Paul Kirk for Olson's aunt and uncle, located 300 feet (91 m) away from Longbranch Cabin. **ABOVE:** Photograph taken by Olson in 1966 during a trip to Luxor Temple in Egypt, which became a lifelong inspiration.

Landscape, too, remains key to the way Olson sees the world around him. Born in St. Louis (though his family was from the Northwest), he moved at a very young age to the rural town of Enumclaw, Washington, where his stepfather ran a lumber company. He found himself surrounded by the forests, and spent his youth with a family who loved—and hiked through—the region's green forests and mountains. As Olson has pointed out, buildings in western Washington State are not surrounded by flat or rolling land that is open to vistas, nor are they generally part of the transformation of the Jeffersonian grid into suburban development. Almost everywhere, places of habitation are carved out of the woods, and almost everywhere the land slopes. Beyond these immediate conditions, you gain glimpses of the ocean and Puget Sound on one side and, on the other, mountain ranges. The volcano of Mount Rainier in particular has become an icon for Olson. Throughout his life he has drawn it obsessively, in every light and condition, as he saw it from Longbranch Cabin. It remains an icon of everything that both nature and his architecture are not: abstract, towering in scale, isolated, and complex in its shape.

What has influenced Olson in his daily practice are the details of the forest, namely the basic shape of conifers. They soar and reach up with very few branches near the base, and are topped by a thin and layered crown. They are unlike the spreading oaks or the shaped willows and other formal trees that have inspired architects elsewhere. Their vertical geometry predominates, and they stand close together in seried ranks. Below them unfold layers of bushes and wildflowers and, below that, lichen and moss. Here, the forest's fabric becomes finer grained, creating layers of textured undergrowth in which you experience moments of transparency, procession, and angled light—elements Olson treasures. He sketches these trees and the plants as inspiration for his architecture, which he sees as a means of drawing attention to this native landscape he loves so well.

Beyond the trees there was always the clearing. The Puget Sound area, where Olson worked almost exclusively for the first decades of his practice, is a liminal space: it is the end of the continent and a landscape where land and sea weave together into peninsulas and islands. Moving through the Sound is a voyage of discovery, with new landscapes and vistas opening up along the water at every turn. There is no sense that there is one thing—the land—and then another—the

OPPOSITE, TOP LEFT: A skylight over the bed frames the sky. **OPPOSITE, TOP RIGHT:** Bedroom addition to Longbranch Cabin made in 1981. View outside from the deck. **OPPOSITE, BOTTOM:** Olson working on a design in his summer office on the beach at Longbranch.

sea, but rather that the two play off each other. As they do so, they create an order, a line, and a moment at which you can see where you are, if even only briefly. It was that push and pull of forms along the line between water and land that gave Olson his central ordering device.

The final condition that has shaped Olson's architecture is his determined and almost single-minded concentration on the design of private homes. When he first started practicing architecture, the office had a varied portfolio of commissions. Their most prominent structure in those early years, the 1978 Pike & Virginia Building in Seattle's historic Pike Place Market, is a mixed-use structure—one of the first of its kind in this part of the world—combining ground-floor retail and apartments. Olson and his wife Katherine lived there for eight years. It consolidated a growing reputation that he and his firm were already making for themselves with thoughtful structures, which would seem to lead them on a more standard path from early residential experiments toward larger civic, commercial, and corporate commissions. Certainly, the Pike & Virginia Building remains a masterpiece in its stripped-down concrete frame, which the architect expressed with clarity—an infill building connected with its industrial and maritime surroundings.

Then, in the early 1980s, when one of the periodic economic recessions that impact architects—often quite severely, and industry-wide—hit Seattle, the firm nearly closed its doors. By this time, Olson had taken on several partners. What kept the firm going were the houses they were designing for clients with enough means to withstand the tumultuous economic tides. In recognizing the stability that residential design offered, Olson and his partners vowed thereafter to maintain a steady stream of residential work, knowing the staying power of this type of architecture. Although he has designed notable civic structures, such as the renovation of St. Mark's Cathedral, the Whatcom Museum's Lightcatcher building, or the Bellevue Botanical Garden Visitor Center, Olson has become a master of private residential design. It is residential architecture that he has been most successful at, and it is these commissions on which he lavishes most of his time and care.

For half a century, Olson has applied his expertise, experience, and studies of history and nature to create a domestic order all his own. A review of his key designs shows how he has

OPPOSITE, TOP: Pike & Virginia Building, Seattle, Washington, 1978. This was the first new building constructed in the Pike Place Market Historic District in fifty years. **OPPOSITE, BOTTOM LEFT:** Living room of Jim and Katherine Olson's condominium on the top floor of the Pike & Virginia Building. **OPPOSITE, BOTTOM RIGHT:** In 1981 Olson, along with a group of architects called "The Gang of Five," imagined several possibilities for the future of downtown Seattle for The Weekly news magazine.

elaborated and refined the continuum of his architecture from the first project to his most recent; in the Conry Residence he designed that faces Longbranch Cabin you can see many of the same elements he explored and refined in his later houses. He received that commission from a longtime friend, Carey Conry—who, when they were teenagers, told him that when he was ready she wanted him to design a house for her. After he obtained his degree from the University of Washington and opened his office in 1965, he called Carey and accepted the commission to design her house.

Olson set the Conry Residence just off the top of the ridge facing the inlet that separates the site from his Longbranch Cabin. A path with several shallow steps leads to a pair of large, crafted wood doors. Above, the roof pops up, lighting the deep-set entry door, which opens to reveal a view straight through the house. Inside, the passage steps down several feet toward the view of the water. The axis continues and pushes out a seating area, which is set in its own glass-enclosed bay window cantilevered over the cliff. Your eye is drawn to this edge as the living spaces open up on either side, suspended as far as the house can reach over the view.

Moving toward that bay window view, another axis opens up on either side. Here, Olson designed the first version of his central spine corridor, which became the defining organizational element not only for his houses, but for nearly all of the civic, cultural, and commercial buildings he has since designed. At the Conry Residence, the spine is partially implied, as an area that slips by the formal dining room, and partially real, as a corridor leading to the master bedroom. It divides the house in two, with the main living areas as open, airy structures reaching out into nature on one side, and the more enclosed and service-oriented rooms behind the dividing line. Already here, Olson is beginning to break apart the home's composition from a centralized structure into a series

OPPOSITE: Jim and Katherine Olson's condominium in Pioneer Square, Seattle, Washington, 1987. The stairwell is an experiment in light.
ABOVE: In the Olson Condominium, the living room is an experiment in art as an environment.

of pavilions, real and implied, along a seam that connects them to each other, and to the view.

The ways in which Olson carried out the details of the Conry Residence hark back to his formal education as well as his work with Paul Kirk and Ralph Anderson. As in many of his later works, the walls of Conry Residence are covered with vertical-grained planks, and the ceiling is a plane lifted up above the support structure, allowing light in through clerestory windows. The actual framing structure sits in front of the walls, making visible what holds the house together and what encloses the space. At times, the detailing seems to come from Olson's desire to create a geometric pattern, as when he frames the panels around the windows with square reliefs that connect the sills, lintels, and eave lines.

Even so, the system that would come to define Olson's architecture was clear in this early project. Later houses would consist of a central axis down the length of the site, or in places where the land broke and started its descent toward the view. The axis would be embedded in the house itself, and thus more modernist than traditional: domestic order was more important than social order. Some later houses offered entry directly on the axis at one of the ends, but in most cases, Olson preferred to develop a cross-axis passage along which one approaches. Quite often that axis would move downward a few steps, so as not to overwhelm visitors with the house's

mass. The entrance line would either continue out to the landscape, or would dissipate into the main living spaces.

Then, the main spaces would move out toward the view from the central spine, leaving the spine to act as a connector. In later houses, this spine would also become a gallery for the display of art. The living areas would be tall, their proportions as elongated as the trees that had inspired Olson since his youth, and this was true even when he was working in very different climates and landscapes. The bedrooms would often be located at the far ends of the axis, with children's and guest wings placed at the opposite ends of the house. The service areas, which in early houses included the kitchen, would then be tucked into the other side of the axis, framing the entrance pathway while staying out of sight.

The vertical proportions of Olson's houses began to dominate, reflecting the tree line outside, not only in the reach of the posts holding up the floating roofs, but also in glass panes and doors, which Olson often stretched beyond traditional dimensions. Against this upward flow, Olson then juxtaposed floating planes, such as light shelves and lower roofs, which simultaneously brought the scale down and made the whole appear more lofty. Only in the private areas of his homes would he step down from that continual upward reach to create places where planes of wood contained and sheltered the view.

The system of detailing within these wood weavings makes it clear how the structure holds together. Olson prefers his beams to slide by his posts, catching them with metal clamps or just letting them sail over with no visible connection point. He uses internal pergolas to create a rhythmic structure that measures one's progress through the spaces; he frames and focuses views by manipulating the sizes of panes of glass. He splits and duplicates posts, ceiling planes, and frames, creating visual echoes and activating their surrounding spaces with their rhythm. Only where he wants the house to continue into nature does he slide the window frames into walls, so that the axes appear to extend into the woods.

Once he set this direction in his houses, Olson then spent the next forty years perfecting his craft. There are very few curves or diagonals in Olson's work, and the axis is always strong.

OPPOSITE: Penfield Residence, Longbranch, Washington, 1968. Olson's second commissioned house in Longbranch, located on the shores of the same bay as the Conry Residence and Longbranch Cabin.

Sometimes his houses develop into L-shapes or other variations of the basic pergola-based plan, but always the order and the structural elements are clear. His architecture continued and perfected many of the themes set at Longbranch and, over the years, they became more elaborate. Over time, he developed a third characteristic that has become central to his work: designing for art collectors. Starting with the commission for the Gallery House in 1984, Olson has designed homes for some of the best art collections in the American West. He had been involved with arts institutions since the beginning of his career, when Seattle was emerging as a hub for American glass art, and later when it became known for contemporary and modern art in general. Olson found inspiration while working on site-specific installations with artists such as James Turrell, and in his own loft in downtown Seattle, which is filled with art and artifacts that he and Katherine have collected over the decades. It is through this appreciation for art that Olson came to the commission for the Gallery House, and from it followed the design of many later homes that house private, premier collections.

Gallery House appears to depart from much of Olson's other work. He designed it at the height of post-modernism, and the firm was as sensitive then to the movement's (fleeting) dominance as they have been to other architectural movements over the years. Gallery House, which sits in an affluent residential neighborhood, is not the assembly of columns, glass cubes, and flat roofs that mark most of Olson's other designs. Rather, it consists of two long spines, each capped with a gabled roof, which run along the site's long ridge. At the front of these is an entry spine that continues along the outside as a rectangular frame, eschewing the differentiation of vertical and horizontal elements so common in the rest of Olson's residential work.

Upon entering the house, after passing by large and forceful works of art, a turn leads to a parallel spine, which has the more traditional (for Olson) function of organizing the house's major

OPPOSITE: Gallery House, Seattle, Washington, 1987. Olson's first home designed for a major art collection. ABOVE: Exterior of Gallery House.

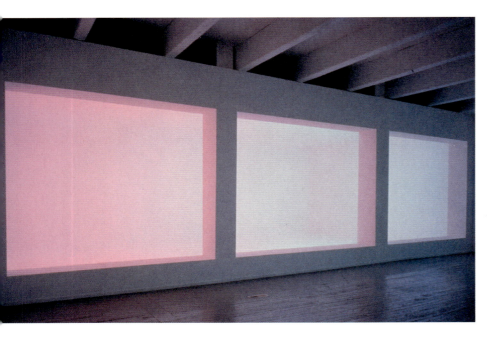

rooms while framing the works of art beneath a gabled skylight hidden above a translucent scrim. Although the ceilings are high, the coves lower the scale in a manner that concentrates your attention on the home's art. The walls are covered in sheetrock and also concrete tiles that surround blond wood frames—it is as if the house's axes and boxes of light were carved out of a solid mass. This house was the first time Olson collaborated with the interior designer Terry Hunziker, who became his collaborator on many other projects; together, they created a muted, monumental surrounding that puts the art first. Even the views across Lake Washington are fragments, with the many windows granting sight only of the small garden outside. At the Gallery House, Olson learned how to focus his architecture on art.

In subsequent designs, he honed that focus even further, learning what colors, proportions, and lighting worked best to preserve and highlight the art. Over time, Olson developed the sense that, when he was designing an art house, what he was really designing was a private museum. However, at the same time, he liberated himself from adapting the forms of public art galleries. He did so most notably at Decorative Arts House in Colorado. There, he stripped down the more solid forms to a grid of painted steel members that created a system of transparent and translucent display cases.

By the early 2000s, Olson was designing more expansive and sophisticated versions of his cabin that contained his clients' art collections. While he was also working for clients who did not have a particular interest in art, it was the collectors' homes in the Pacific Northwest that solidified his reputation and evidenced his skill in connecting art, nature, and people. The most notable designs of this middle period are An American Place and the House of Light, both in Seattle.

An American Place is one of Olson's most sophisticated and assured compositions. It also contains one of the most impressive collections his work has ever housed. The home's entry

ABOVE: In 1982, Olson assisted with drawings and installation for artist James Turrell's first major exhibit in Seattle at CoCA, the Center on Contemporary Art. Turrell has had a lasting influence on Olson's work. OPPOSITE, TOP LEFT: Courtyard at Bluff House, Seattle, Washington, 1992. OPPOSITE, TOP RIGHT: Interior of Fryberger Floating Home, Seattle, Washington, 1976. OPPOSITE, BOTTOM: West Wall Remodel of St. Mark's Episcopal Cathedral, Seattle, Washington, 1997. The reredos, pictured, was a collaboration with artist Ed Carpenter.

sequence begins along a walkway covered by a steel canopy cantilevered from a line of concrete columns that march down one side of the path, their bases planted in a shallow pool. This rare bit of asymmetry, matched only by Olson's tendency to place a chimney to one side of the entry, offers a sense of shelter without closing off views of nature.

Entering through a tall and airy vestibule, the gallery axis is anchored by four concrete columns that support an intricate system of wood and metal beams sliding past each other. This space both reinforces the entry axis and extends the order out along the house's main path. In this home, the grand scale and refined materials are more reminiscent of a contemporary art gallery than a private home, but Olson loosens the whole by balancing the steel beams on the columns' corners and filling in their profiles with wood. The ceiling appears to float above that structural web, while the walls of glass providing views of Lake Washington defer to the structure, interfering as little as possible with your contemplation of the outside. Beneath and inside this architecture, works by Georgia O'Keeffe, Jasper Johns, and Willem de Kooning shine forth.

Beyond the rooms that flank the central crossing, An American Place becomes quieter. To the right of the living area is the master bedroom complex, off of which extends a pavilion toward the lake. To the left is a separate wing containing guest rooms, which you access through glass-enclosed corridors; along the path a Franz Kline hangs at one end and a Marsden at the other. In the home's private realms, the ceiling gently descends and plaster walls take over from the articulated structure, making one feel more at home.

The sense of clarity and framing achieved in An American Place is seamless. These elements reinforce a sense of order and visual concentration—emphasizing that this is a place of shelter built for both art and people, and one that weaves together the human life and artworks it contains. There is no room for confusion. You can marvel endlessly at the intricacy of how the place fits

OPPOSITE, TOP LEFT: Red House, Denver, Colorado, 1998. This art collector's residence is located in LoDo, Denver's historic district. OPPOSITE, TOP RIGHT: Interior of Decorative Arts House, Denver, Colorado, 2008. OPPOSITE, BOTTOM: Gallery hallway of Garden House, Atherton, California, 1998. ABOVE: Architecture frames art at An American Place, Hunts Point, Washington, 2004.

together, while always knowing where you are in relation to the axes and the outside.

This degree of clarity is just as strong in the House of Light, although its detailing is lighter and more ethereal. This is somewhat paradoxical, because there are actually more walls—at least in the house's central part—than there are in An American Place. At the House of Light, the whole composition is more compact, although it is not much smaller in scale.

Like An American Place, the entrance to the House of Light occurs in the middle of its central axis. In this case, the house sits quite far away and downslope from the main road, so that you wind through gardens and past a Richard Serra sculpture before arriving at what is nearly the main axis's end. The path continues, as always, out to a back lawn—and, once again, to Lake Washington, but here, the cross-axis does not open up. Rather, it terminates in something more like a tall art gallery, with cream-colored walls on either side and a wood ceiling above. Then, the space opens in its middle to reveal a much taller plane and a scrim-covered skylight that bathes the gallery in the light that gives the house its name.

This space is as much an art gallery as the central area of An American Place, but at the House of Light, the living areas are less insistent on the art's primacy. Its high ceilings are covered with wood and open in the center to reveal not light, but more wood beams. Lower soffits bring down the scale, while solid walls block most of what would be otherwise overwhelming views of Lake Washington. Here, the dining area and den are arranged at the front side of the house, and together, the semi-public areas form a rectangular block around the art gallery.

To the left of the entrance is a smaller pavilion, its forms as symmetrical, but stepped in plan, as they are in the living area. Here, there are guest rooms and offices, but also the House of Light's

ABOVE: Landscape frames architecture frames art at the House of Light, Medina, Washington, 2005.
OPPOSITE, LEFT: Lake House, Mercer Island, Washington, 2003. The sculptural form exhausts hot air to cool the house naturally. **OPPOSITE, RIGHT:** Reflecting pool at Ocean House, Island of Hawaii, 2003.

showstopper: a site-specific installation by the artist James Turrell, which fills the central area at the end of the main axis. Continually changing in hue, it is a place of contemplation and wonder that just happens to be located in the house's core. In Turrell's skyspace, the beauty of light is honed and focused—a highly manipulated play on the house's name that draws attention to the source even in its artifice.

In recent years, Olson has moved beyond the roots of his native Northwest, designing buildings in California, Hawaii, New York, and Washington, D.C., but also in South Korea, Indonesia, Hong Kong, London, and Mexico. His expanded horizons have played an evolutionary role in the idiom or character of his houses—Chinese proportions are evident in the Shek O House in Hong Kong, while both the Desert House in Palm Desert and a recent house on Mexico's Baja Peninsula make reference to the tradition of building heavier, heat-absorbing structures in these arid climates—he has kept the basic organizing principles that are at work in all of his houses.

This blend of experience and adaptation in Olson's work is evident in the design of two of his most recently completed houses: the Bay Area Hill House in Marin County, and the California Meadow House south of San Francisco. These two homes are the result of the Bay Area's booming economy in recent decades, and thus are both quite large—they employ all of the methods that Olson has developed to create semi-public realms in relation to the outside that impress and even overwhelm, as well as private areas within and around these spaces that comfortably house the inhabitants.

The Bay Area Hill House, for instance, has a spectacular view from its hilltop site out across San Francisco Bay to the city. Olson's house, of course, does not defer to that vista, but captures and reveals it over time and in discrete moments as you move through the space. The house's central gallery is located at its middle, but you reach that point by first traveling up a gradual set of stairs that lead to an aedicule—a small, temple-like structure with four metal posts that creates a centering effect. To the right is one of Olson's classic long axes, whose length he marks with periodic repetitions of the first four posts, only these are concrete columns. These columns hold up the side ledges, which serve to reduce the scale, as is usual in his buildings. A wood ceiling hovers above lines of clerestories, drawing light into the art-filled space. At the end you can see a sculpture and catch a glimpse of the nearby hills, but the real views are at ninety degrees from this line, past the main living areas that step down the slope toward a lawn and the views of San Francisco beyond.

The living areas in this home are more compact than those of Olson's other art houses; extending out and down, they span between two outdoor staircases that provide access to the lawn. On one side is the master bedroom compound and, on the other, a children's wing anchored by a communal play area with a hidden loft. In this home, the service areas are below ground,

while a yoga studio and offices are located in a separate pavilion to the north, across a courtyard. This outdoor space is bounded by an extension of one of the cross-axes to the west and the wall of the lap pool on a higher terrace.

By the time he had completed these homes, which were multi-year projects, Olson had developed several sophisticated variations on the articulation of vertical and horizontal axes that have been his obsession since he built his Longbranch Cabin. What started out as posts there and in the Conry Residence, then split apart into paired beams in later designs—so that you could understand them as part of an overall weave and so that they could have an active relation with the space around them—have developed into a family of vertical structures. Today, when Olson wants to go high and dramatic, as in the entrance of the Bay Area Hill House, the columns become light steel posts. When he is creating spaces for art or formal reception, they often become smooth concrete squares, without bases or capitals. In between, Olson's vertical elements transform simple wood posts into marriages of wood and steel. At the windows these compositions become delicate fins that point outward while supporting massive overhangs that shade the glass from rain and sun. These contrast with the interior ceilings, which float as layers separated by clerestories or hidden light shelves, allowing them to slide by each other to open up what is above, rather than feeling like a weight.

Between these pieces of structure and below the floating ceilings, the architect carefully places walls, which are no more the final ends of spaces than the ceilings are. They are partitions on which

OPPOSITE: Swimming pool at Hong Kong Villa, Hong Kong, 2008. Colors and materials reflect and grow out of the environment. **ABOVE, LEFT:** Desert House, Palm Desert, California, 1999. The front door is made of thirty glass tiles hand-crafted by artist Dan Dailey. **ABOVE, RIGHT:** At Desert House, materials blend with the natural environment.

to hang art, and ways to channel movement from one space to another. Only in the most private areas do they close off rooms completely or provide acoustic and visual privacy. They are often clad with wood, creating a gentle, cocoon-like isolation from the grandeur in and outside the house.

For all the articulation of structure, room, and view, what is remarkable in Olson's most recent homes is the way in which major structural components seem to dissolve or disappear. For decades, it seems, the architect has worked at smoothing out the sorts of details that catch the eye in his original cabin, where, as he admits, you can find many marks in the wood where his hammer missed nails. Now, when you inspect the joint where a wall meets a column or a corner, it is impossible to find the bolts, angles, or flanges that make these seams come together with such precision. Nor are any of the electrical, plumbing, or air-handling elements visible. It is only upon close examination that you discover the vents where air flows in and out of spaces. Recent works such as the Bay Area Hill House are essays in the seamlessness of detail, as well as axis, space, and connection, the foregrounding of views, the display of art—and, most of all, living. The mechanics and joinery are contained within the walls, behind the axes, or tucked into places that only the construction drawings reveal.

If Olson's Bay Area Hill House is grand and self-confident in command of its hilltop site, the California Meadow House points the way toward the more ethereal side of his architecture. Its main rooms dance around the spine with a freedom that emerges in the best of this architect's work; three of these types of spaces becoming separate buildings that step back from that central axis. The home's roofs float high above the living areas, where the panes of glass are quite

large, in one case lowering into the ground so that it disappears completely. Here, Olson approaches architecture that goes beyond the roots of Longbranch Cabin and becomes "almost nothing"—as the modernist master Ludwig Mies van der Rohe believed his art could be.

The entrance to the California Meadow House occurs at the end of its gallery, stepping down as water cascades to the left then disappears upon entering the massive door, only to reappear later as a long reflecting pool at the far end of the axis. Olson has here given up the columns in the home's central axis, leaving the walls and the openings between them to create the necessary rhythm to affect a sense of progression when you move down and through the house. The spaces here are more functionally mixed and more formally syncopated than in Olson's earlier houses, with an open kitchen integrated into the main living area and a second living area that looks out to the swimming pool and the hills beyond. You can sense the breakdown in the kind of formality that might otherwise appear alien to these younger, Silicon Valley-oriented clients. Family life dominates, and its messier, more energetic rhythms actually serve to free up the home's spaces.

The house's physical structure is equally relaxed, resolving into walls covered in plaster, large panes of glass without the insistent grid of mullions so common in many contemporary house designs, and with floating ceilings unanchored by coves and transoms. Instead of columns, there are the fins; rather than beams, there are slats.

The California Meadow House does have a monumental or semi-public side and function: the owners entertain and hold fundraisers there quite often. However, Olson has separated these areas into three pavilions connected underground. They flank the entrance and include a dining space whose walls disappear so that the area can be opened completely to the terrace in front, a meeting space that can seat several dozen for a formal dinner, and a guest house. A bar and

OPPOSITE: At the House of Light, horizontal sunshades protect the art and recall the horizontality of the landscape. **ABOVE:** Glass Apartment, Seattle, Washington, 2001. The bathtub becomes an art piece of handmade glass crafted by Peter David.

home theater, as well as service spaces, are situated beneath these more public entertaining spaces. Instead of holding onto the notion that the house's formal characteristics and functions must be integrated, Olson has freed them to be separate and stated in the simplest possible manner.

As Jim Olson builds on his five decades of designing such grand homes, the scale, scope, and reach of his work becomes ever larger. His design of a residence for a client in Jakarta, Indonesia, is actually a family compound, like a resort or village in scope and layout. The strength of the architect's work is that he can control the spaces and the details, the structure, and the character of these houses at seemingly any scale and in any location. He can make areas feel homey and monumental, make you understand where you are and how it all fits together, make the rooms float, open, and close with skill, and combine them into carefully choreographed spaces.

As Olson applies the skills he learned from designing houses to more public buildings, such as the Lightcatcher at the Whatcom Museum in Bellingham and the Foss Waterway and Seaport in Tacoma, both in Washington; the Kirkland Museum in Denver, Colorado; and the Jordan Schnitzer Museum of Art at Washington State University in Pullman, he continues to experiment. In buildings such as Foss, which includes the last historic vestiges of what was once a mile-long warehouse structure, he turns the space into a refined version of its functional predecessor. Building on his work with James Turrell, Olson is exploring ways of painting spaces with light and new materials in the WSU Museum of Art. In some cases, as in the Bellevue Botanical Gardens Visitor Center, he even adapts his residential design methodology directly to a public education building and visitor space, cladding the pavilions with wood to create a series of intimate, linked experiences that he strings along a central axis that you enter in its middle.

At the core of Olson's experimentation remains the residential realm; it is his small structures that, starting—and continuing—with Longbranch Cabin, show him at his most inventive. In the later additions to Longbranch, he returns with design strategies devised for his larger commissions. Today, the master bedroom of his cabin is a refined and scaled-down version of bedrooms he has designed for clients: frameless windows that open to the outside and smooth walls hide many of the house's earlier quirks.

OPPOSITE: Glass Farmhouse, Oregon, 2008. The building floats on the field like a boat and reinvents traditional barn forms.

What continues to surprise about Olson's work is his use of rough-and-ready materials. From the beginning, he used simple lumber in his projects and tried different ways of connecting elements. He has continued that experimentation, now also using galvanized metal columns between which he slots standard bits of lumber; connecting pieces of wood with Z-shaped flanges, also made out of galvanized metal; sliding walls by each other to extend forms; cantilevering roofs above as canopies with rough metal member supports. He pushes and pulls rooms off the axis, tumbles them downhill, and opens spaces to the forest and water in any way he can manage. As a body of experiments, Olson's evolving Longbranch Cabin and his smaller works are a concatenation of details that make walking through them a voyage of discovery.

At times, this simplicity resolves itself into simple forms, such as that of the Glass Farmhouse, a one-room structure that stands in the wheat fields of eastern Oregon on a small concrete plinth. Its roof is a single-sloped plane that kinks up toward the views, while a single ledge at the front brings the scale down and shelters inhabitants from the sun. The interior space is a loft in which Olson has reduced the structure to a thin lattice of steel, while the walls and ceiling become sheets of wood of the most elemental sort. It is a radically simplified version of the central spaces of Decorative Arts House. This is Olson's architecture at its most elemental: a primitive hut in the

middle of the prairie. It is also an undressed and abstracted version of the adjacent barn, converting the functional and the closed into a place of contemplation and articulation.

The timber construction at the heart of Olson's work is most clearly evident in City Cabin, a small house he designed as an urban retreat for one of his longtime friends and a Longbranch neighbor. Set on a small lot in a dense Seattle neighborhood, the house presents a closed face to the street. The house's solar collectors and grass roof, both requested by the client, recall the sod roof of Penfield House, designed by Olson in 1968 just down the bend from his Longbranch Cabin. Likewise, the home's rough vertical timbers appear as broad versions of the original siding of Longbranch Cabin.

The central volume of City Cabin—an airy living, cooking, and dining space—contains tall walls of bookshelves made from more rough timber beneath a ceiling of laminated wood beams and standard timbers lifted by pairs of galvanized metal posts over a line of clerestory windows. The wall of glass that faces the library walls opens an expansive view of the back garden interrupted only by one of the paired vertical supports. Although the materials are rough and the space is simple, the detailing is as refined as Olson and his team could make it—from the way beams slide by posts to the manner in which the broad glass panels fill in the space with light and the metal caps protect the laminated beam ends from the rain, while also giving a counterpoint rhythm to the stretch of wood beams.

Like most of Olson's residences, there is, of course, a central axis that runs through City Cabin, albeit abbreviated and partially implied given the lot size. It runs through the street side of the main living space, past the kitchen to a series of service spaces and a guest bedroom anchoring the end. On the other side, to the right of the entry, the central axis leads to the master bedroom, which opens to the garden, while its dressing area and bathroom, in good Olson fashion, are tucked toward the rear of the spine. What makes the master bedroom especially remarkable is that the architect has simplified and strengthened the sense of cocooning by cladding its walls and ceilings with a plywood whose patterns are as lush as those of marble.

Olson Kundig office, Seattle, Washington, 2016. Jim Olson leads the firm along with four co-owners, but the success of each project depends on the collaborative effort of the immensely creative minds that collectively define Olson Kundig.

City Cabin is the distillation of Olson's best houses in miniature, and in affordable materials. He could only have designed it to such a degree of perfection after decades of developing his design approach and the understanding of composition, detailing, and materiality that his residential architecture is known for. This small home also demonstrates that his work does not depend on large budgets and sites, however well he is able to use those to their full effect elsewhere. It is a system for housing that creates a line of order, assigns places for the rooms containing and measuring the activities of everyday life, and then makes the architecture that brings this all together evident in beautiful construction and composition.

"I am a weaver," Olson says of his work. His tapestry consists of structure that is not hierarchical, but is layered vertically and horizontally; of rooms that flow together, weaving in and out of the central axis; and of houses that everywhere bring views of the outside in, while extending the house into nature. It is his particular ability to create a fabric of wood and other simple materials that makes this architect's work so remarkable.

RECENT PROJECTS

CAPITAL HOUSE

LOCATION: WASHINGTON, D.C., USA

COMPLETED: 2008

The client was a single man and a high-energy civil rights lawyer—he served in the US government under Attorney General Janet Reno. He had a specific vision for his house: he wanted a vaulted roof, and he wanted the master bedroom on the second floor under this vault. Inspired by classical monuments such as the Lincoln Memorial at the nearby Capitol, the house is at once monumental and cozy, regal and understated.

I traveled to Washington, D.C. in midsummer to meet the client and see the site for the first time. We spent the entire, very hot day outdoors at the site with a measuring tape, and actually laid out the house that day, exactly as it now stands. That evening we visited the Lincoln Memorial and talked about the power of monumental architecture—the colonnade in the house was a response to this monumentality.

The contemporary lines of this modern residence are balanced by neutral tones and natural materials, including stone, concrete, and bronze. The two-story house is clad in slabs of limestone on the bottom level, rising to extensive glazing on the second story and a curved roof floating above. Not wanting the house to stand out in the traditional neighborhood, we chose dark colors for the exterior that were rich, but would also recede visually.

This house also presents various recurring ideas—indoor/outdoor flow, "magic window," infinite ceiling, and natural materials. The departure here from my usual themes came in the form of the vaulted roof. The house emphasizes scale and proportion, and rooms in the house are arranged as "alcoves" off a grand hallway. The simple C-shaped plan surrounds a private and contemplative central courtyard, which includes a small bamboo garden and a covered lap pool.

The entrance to the house is through a steel and glass vestibule demarcated by an oak door with bronze inlays. Upon entering, one immediately arrives in the main spine of the home, with doors and windows leading out to the courtyard on the left, and the kitchen and office extending to the right. The monumental hallway lined with concrete columns terminates in the formal dining and living rooms, which are complemented by a large stone fireplace and dramatic vaulted ceiling in the living area that appears to dissolve into the sky. Upstairs, crossing a bridge leads to the open master suite, with a series of additional bedrooms down the main hallway. The design incorporates several pieces from the owner's collection of civil rights-inspired art. Artist Scott Fife created a contemporary sculptural portrait of the iconic Supreme Court Justice Thurgood Marshall especially for this house.

PAGE 40: The Longbranch Chair designed by Jim Olson on the deck at Longbranch Cabin. PRECEDING PAGES: Living room pavilion with lap pool in the foreground. OPPOSITE, TOP: The steel and glass entry vestibule extends out from the main facade. OPPOSITE, BOTTOM LEFT: An oak and bronze front door marks the home's threshold. OPPOSITE, BOTTOM RIGHT: The lap pool bounds the home's inner courtyard. ABOVE: Main level plan.

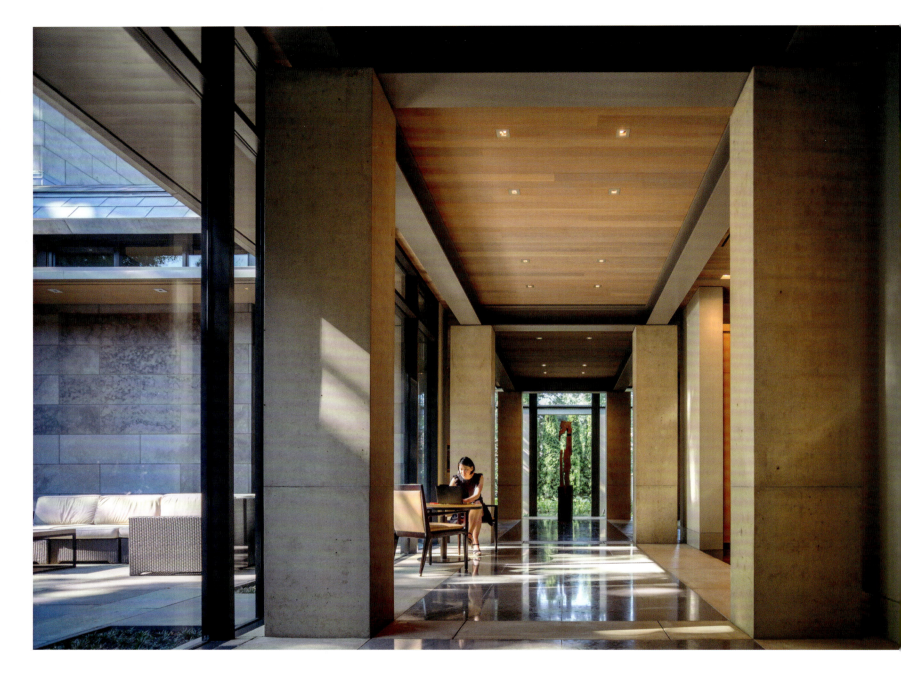

ABOVE: Concrete columns line the formal circulation spine that connects the rooms together.
At the end is a sculpture by Jorge Yàzpik. **OPPOSITE:** Living room seen from dining room.
OVERLEAF: Courtyard looking toward living room pavilion.

LIGHTCATCHER AT
THE WHATCOM MUSEUM

LOCATION: BELLINGHAM, WASHINGTON, USA

COMPLETED: 2009

For this building, my competition-winning design concept was to gather light in a region where natural light is not abundant, especially in winter—so we made a huge wall of translucent glass that would glow like an agate on a Northwest beach. I wanted to soften light like our clouds, and create a sense of mystery like our mist and fog. This light-gathering wall would also curve to respond to the path of the sun during the day, and enclose a large space within, playing off the loft spaces inside the simple building, and providing just the kind of urban gathering space Bellingham needed.

The Lightcatcher wall, 37 feet (11 m) high and 176 feet (54 m) long, is at the physical center of the project, gently curving to form a spacious exterior courtyard, while connecting the museum's interior and exterior spaces. During daylight hours, the light-porous wall floods the halls and galleries inside with a warm luminosity, serving as an elegant and energy-saving light fixture.

The curved glass wall of the Lightcatcher is also a passive heating and cooling device: its double-glazed skin keeps interior spaces cool via the stack effect, and in cooler weather, vents at the top of the wall can be closed and radiant energy is captured within, insulating the building.

The first floor of the building features a lobby, three galleries (one of which is double-height), and an interactive children's learning space, as well as other amenities. The building's second floor houses an additional exhibition gallery, meeting and classroom space, and museum offices. The single-story lobby is topped by a 3,000-square-foot (279 sq m) green roof, which features an interpretive exhibit about the roof and low-impact development strategies. The building utilizes natural materials endemic to the region.

Outside, the Lightcatcher reflects light into the Garden of the Ancients, where landscape architect Charles Anderson placed a ginkgo tree, a species that has survived from the time of the dinosaurs. The 7,000-square-foot (650 sq m) courtyard is designed as a civic gathering space and a dynamic backdrop for sculpture. In the evening it glows with the colors of the structure's interior illumination and, like a lantern, it acts as a warm and welcoming beacon to the community. Pedestrians can view the courtyard—and the art and activities within—through large openings to the street, ensuring the museum is as active outside as it is inside.

PRECEDING PAGES: Public gathering in courtyard. **OPPOSITE:** Building entry with view into courtyard beyond. **ABOVE:** Ground-floor plan.

ABOVE: The glass wall naturally illuminates interior circulation areas and warms the space on cold days. **OPPOSITE:** The glass wall curves to create an outdoor community gathering space.

LIGHTCATCHER AT THE WHATCOM MUSEUM

BELOW: Sculptures by artist John Grade hang from the 25-foot-high (8 m) ceiling of the special exhibition space. **OPPOSITE:** The circulation space is naturally heated and ventilated by the double-layered glass wall.

MEXICO BEACH HOUSE

LOCATION: SAN JOSÉ DEL CABO, BAJA, MEXICO

COMPLETED: 2010

I've known the client for over fifty years, since high school; in fact, our parents had been friends since college around 1930. I did two family houses for her while in my twenties, and the design process for this house was effortless: we knew each other's tastes.

Set on a sandy beach in Mexico, this is a seasonal vacation house for the client and her extended family of four children and many grandchildren. It enables the owner to accommodate family and friends while also maintaining a comfortable private space. A central, two-story gathering space—living, dining, kitchen, and catering—is separate from the master suite off to one side. An upstairs floor containing bedrooms, bunkrooms, bathrooms, and a kids' area can be closed off, maintaining an intimate feel. The whole ocean-side living room window wall slides open, so inside becomes outside—this is the perfect climate for outdoor living. There are multiple outdoor living spaces around the house, as well as deep, cantilevered overhangs. Sustainable features include solar thermal panels and natural ventilation.

This is a modern home that is influenced by local traditions and the natural environment. The stone and stucco used in the building are the color of sand. Dark wood beams recall historic Mexican buildings and colonial houses inspired by Spanish architecture. The shutters can be closed for privacy while still allowing a breeze to flow through. There is a vista right through from the entry to the ocean, and a floating trellis supported by columns leads the way. Interior designer Terry Hunziker, who did the furniture, had also worked with me and with the client many times. We all enjoyed the congenial ease of the design process due to our longtime relationships with one another.

PRECEDING PAGES: View into living room from swimming pool. **OPPOSITE, TOP:** Inspired by traditional Mexican design, the house is nonetheless modern, weaving together a tapestry of travertine, wood, and integrally colored plaster. **OPPOSITE, BOTTOM:** A view from the entry gate runs the length of the home to the ocean beyond.

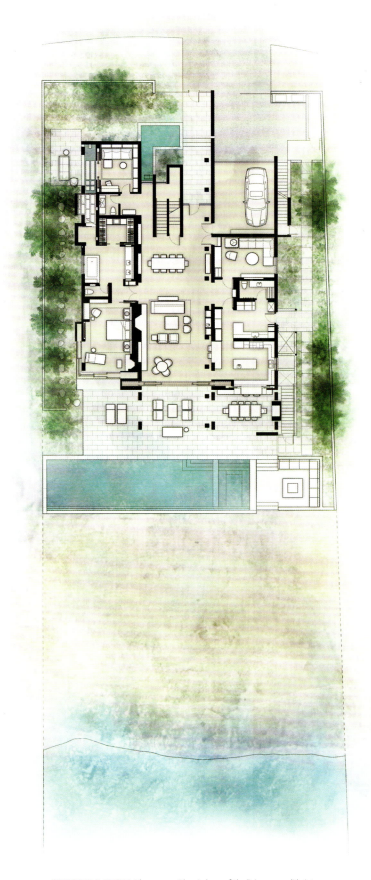

PRECEDING PAGES: The ocean-side windows of the living room slide into the wall, opening the room to the ocean. **OPPOSITE:** An overhead trellis shades the outdoor seating area from intense sun. **ABOVE:** Ground-floor plan.

NORTHWOODS HOUSE

LOCATION: IRON RIVER, MICHIGAN, USA

COMPLETED: 2010

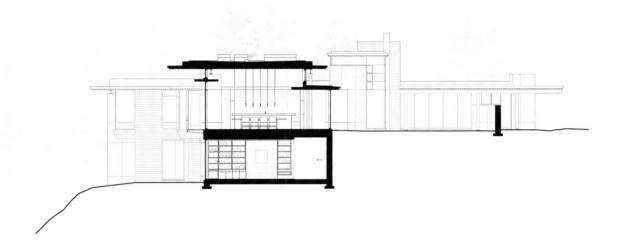

This home on a lake in Michigan's Upper Peninsula frames and emphasizes its natural context, making nature its focus. The design reacts to the surrounding environment, dissolving inside/outside boundaries and creating composed views into the woods and toward the water.

The clients were reticent to contact me at first because theirs wasn't a large project, and it is in a remote location. But they sent pictures of amazing concrete houses in Mexico and South America, which I loved, and I also loved the site—a place I'd never been before. The clients' enthusiasm for architecture inspired the design process, but one puzzle was how to translate inspirations from tropical climates to a place that was freezing cold and covered with snow in winter. A significant part of the design was to harvest sunshine for light and warmth in winter—by facing south, using clerestories and skylights, and using light colors.

The house is organized on the site in two directions. An east–west axis creates a path from the front door to a lake view, while floor-to-ceiling windows along a north–south axis frame the surrounding garden and forest. A sculptural staircase anchors the intersection of the two main axes. Throughout the interior, ceiling heights and room volumes vary, and rooms become more spacious as they open toward views. Roof extensions and light shelves create clear definition between vertical spaces. The orderly axis breaks down outside the house, as an asymmetrical cantilevered roof directs the gaze to the woods and lake views to the west.

In such a remote location, most cooking is done at home, and the kitchen is therefore the focus of daily life. The kitchen, living, and dining areas are all in one room. Family and guests gather either at the kitchen counter or around the fireplace.

Wilderness is the focus from the rooms in every direction, and we designed the interiors and also the dining table. Landscape architect Steven Stimson created gardens that took the lines of the concrete structure out into the landscape. This reflects my own philosophy that landscape architecture, interiors, and art are all one environment. Exterior materials will weather over time to match the surroundings, while colors in the interior are inspired by the landscape—for example, an interior wood stain matches the color of the bark of nearby trees.

PRECEDING PAGES: View of house from the south. OPPOSITE, TOP: The open-plan kitchen, dining, and living area is the heart of this family home, anchored by a custom-designed dining table. Warm south sunlight is brought into the north wall of the kitchen through hidden skylights. OPPOSITE, BOTTOM: Custom features like the front door and a fabric lampshade add to the unique quality of the house. ABOVE: Cross-section looking north through living, dining, and kitchen area.

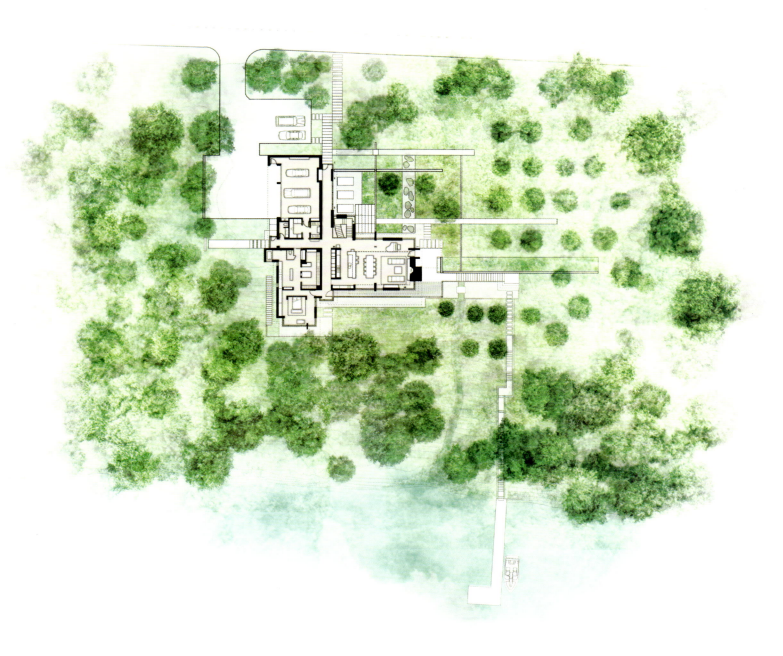

PRECEDING PAGES: Looking into living room from kitchen. **ABOVE:** Main level plan.
OPPOSITE, TOP: Elements of the architecture weave the home into the landscape.
OPPOSITE, BOTTOM: At the end of every hallway is a framed and focused view.

BELOW: The master bedroom is like a refuge overlooking the woods and lake below.

OPPOSITE: The master bath flows seamlessly from the master bedroom.

PAVILION HOUSE

LOCATION: BELLEVUE, WASHINGTON, USA

COMPLETED: 2011

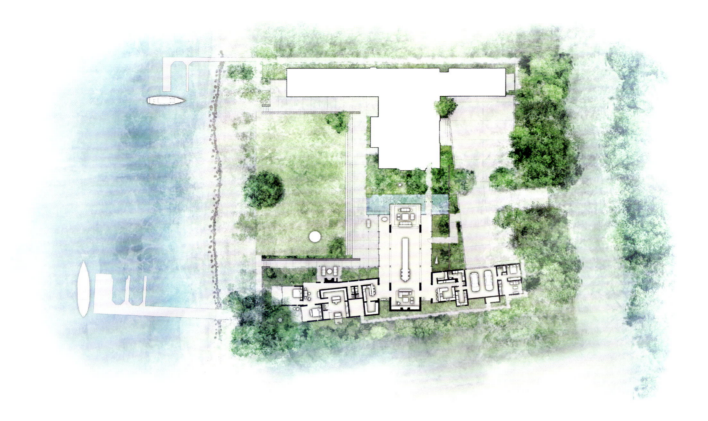

The clients wanted a bigger house and, having looked all around the Seattle/Bellevue area, decided they liked their own neighborhood best, so they bought the property next door in order to expand the house in which they had raised their family. The Pavilion House is therefore situated on a west-facing waterfront site adjacent to the clients' existing home.

The new area of the residence is intended to complement the original home, not necessarily mimic the style. The estate functions as a home for the family, as well as a venue for entertaining large groups. The clients had started a collection of Northwest contemporary art, and I helped them select artists, and advised on site-specific pieces. The collection expanded to encompass mid-century Northwest masters and also historic Native American baskets. As in all of my houses, the site and the landscape, the architectural interiors, and the art are one unified design/environment.

The addition was a room to host large gatherings, so it needed to be comfortable for anywhere between two and two hundred people. We created a large space but at a human scale and with warm colors, with an intimate seating area at each end. One end is open to the garden for summer and daytime, and the other is enclosed, with a fireplace for winter and evenings.

The large table, designed by Garret Cord Werner, is the centerpiece of the space. It is a multi-purpose table that can accommodate dinner parties, work, basket exhibits—and many hors d'oeuvres at parties.

The light coming into the space is balanced, from a skylight and glazing on both sides of the room—intended to let the indoors and outdoors flow together. Sliding glass doors allow the main space to be open to the outdoors on warm days. We worked with landscape architect Charles Anderson to create a huge lakeside lawn, a "commons" framed by the two L-shaped houses, perfect for games or outdoor gatherings.

PRECEDING PAGES: View of the new wing from the porch of the original home. The two wings frame the lawn, which contains a sculpture by Bernard Hosey. **ABOVE:** Floor plan of Pavilion House adjacent to the footprint of the original home. **OPPOSITE:** Exterior and interior artworks are woven into the fabric of the architecture, including a rusted steel garden sculpture by Peter Millett.

PRECEDING PAGES: The sitting area at the north end of the living room feels at one with the garden. **OPPOSITE:** A custom table by Garret Cord Werner functions equally well as a dining table for large gatherings and as a display table for the couple's collection of Northwest art. **ABOVE:** The north sitting area, elevated above the surrounding finished floor, cantilevers over a water feature.

SEOUL SHOPS

LOCATION: SEOUL, REPUBLIC OF KOREA

COMPLETED: 2012

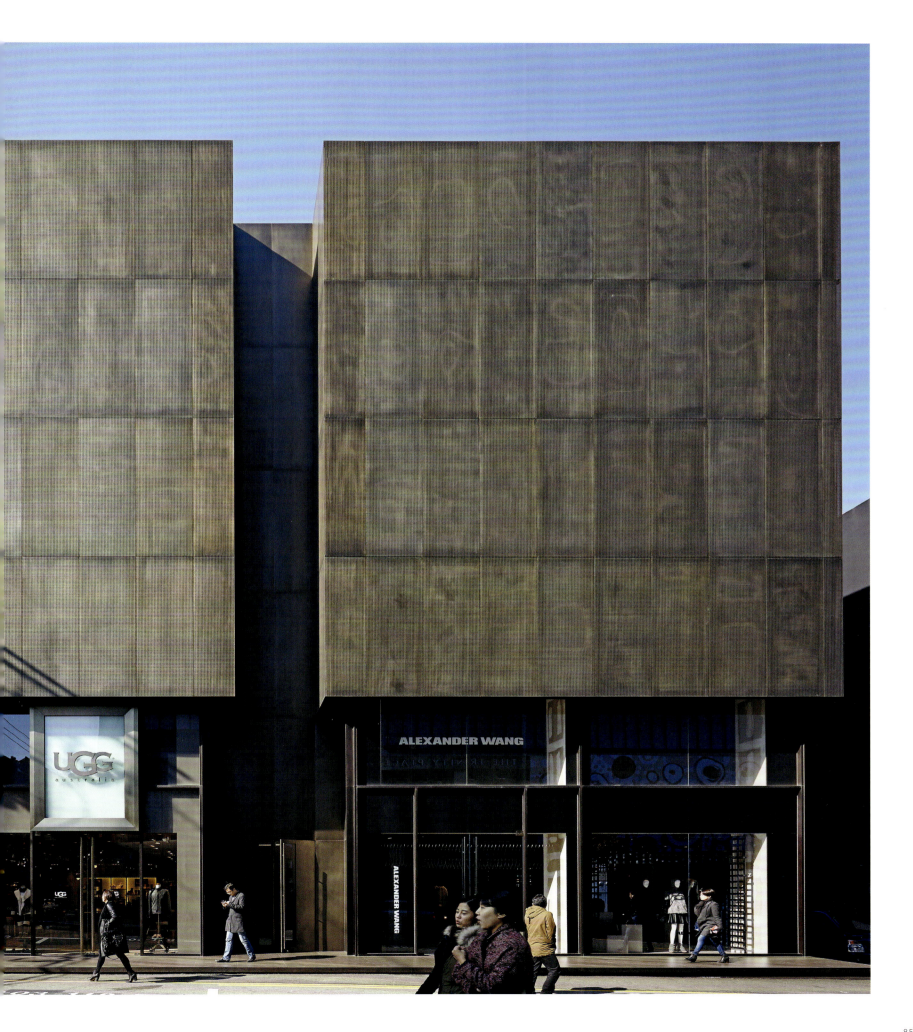

This scheme involved the redesign of a facade, breathing new life into an existing building on one of Seoul's most popular shopping streets. The fashionable shopping neighborhood surrounding the building is home to abundant "look at me" buildings, vying to attract attention to the high-profile brands housed within. My idea for making a statement in the context of this "ambitious" neighborhood was therefore to take the opposite approach—to aim for a quiet elegance that stands alone by virtue of not trying so hard. The understated power of work by artists such as Donald Judd, Mark Rothko, and James Turrell inspires me, and I consider the finished building to be a reflection of my general philosophy—"quiet" overcomes "noise," eventually.

The original building was redbrick, squat, and rather unattractive—so I posed the question: "How could we make this building elegant?" We had one of our weekly Olson Kundig crits, at which many members of our firm presented their ideas for the building facade. One scheme, by Jeff Ocampo, broke the squat shape into two, producing two halves, each with beautiful proportions. In this way, one rather ordinary shape became two much more elegant shapes. The resulting strong, subtle expression of form balances the lively activity of the retail shops and mixed-use space contained within. The four-story building is currently occupied by UGG and Alexander Wang on the first and second stories, with private office facilities on the third and fourth stories.

We sheathed the building in a bronze-colored "screen" through which you can barely see the outline of the old building behind. The new facade is made from perforated metal panels that seem to float—horizontally away from the existing building, and vertically above the street, which allows the retail spaces below to become the focus. These perforated metal panels also extend above the original building, creating an external, courtyard-like setting that can potentially be used as a rooftop garden in which to relax, a runway for showing clothing collections, or for outdoor gatherings.

PRECEDING PAGES: The facade is broken into two parts, giving each shop a clear identity while creating more vertical proportions. **OPPOSITE:** Nestled between the two facade halves, the entrance to the main building is recessed from the street, keeping the emphasis on the shops.

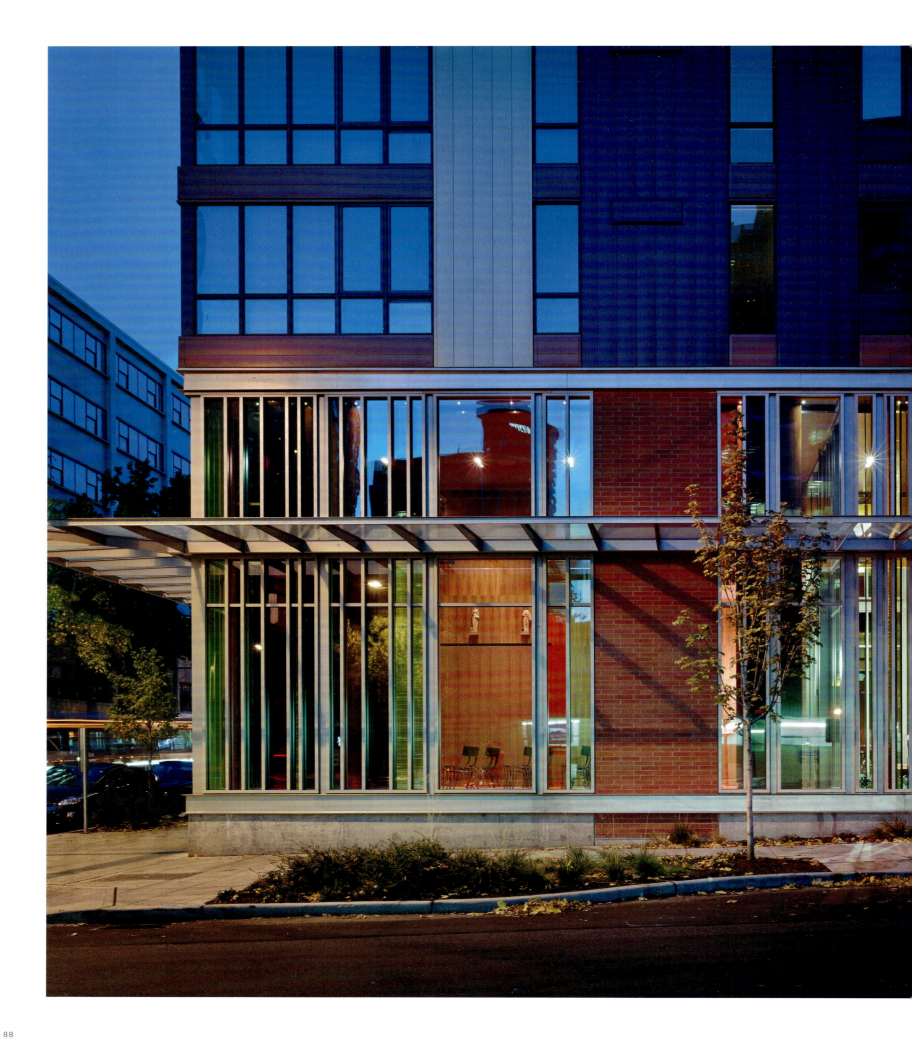

GETHSEMANE CHAPEL

LOCATION: SEATTLE, WASHINGTON, USA

COMPLETED: 2012

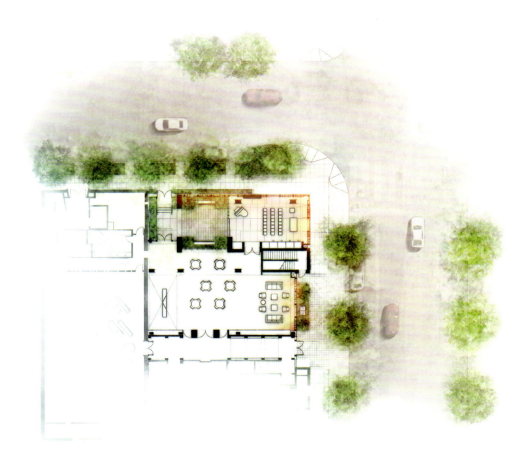

This project is an addition to a 1950s church building, built on the site of one of the oldest churches in Seattle, with an older congregation, some of whom are in their nineties and more. Inspired by small chapels such as St-Chapelle in Paris, the design for this richly complex project enhances the Gethsemane Lutheran Church's already significant presence in the city. We designed the building's exterior and remodeled the church's main sanctuary, as well as the design of the chapel, garden, and the Parish Life Center.

The church had earlier sold half of its property to fund the redevelopment and further its mission of helping underprivileged people living in the downtown area. Low-cost housing units are provided above the church, with social services, many of which are for women with children, housed in the basement. Executive architect SMR led the design of the affordable housing and social service portions of the project.

Our goal was to offer inspiration and refuge in the heart of the city. Near the entrance to the church stands a statue of Christ, creating a "sidewalk chapel" for passersby. The small meditation garden next to the chapel represents the Garden of Gethsemane (the site of Christ's Last Supper), and balances openness with outreach. Both chapel and garden are visible from the street, welcoming people in—and at night they are lit up, like a glowing beacon. Colored glass in the chapel, crafted by Peter David, fits with the Lutheran tradition but is modern in expression. Sunlight projects colors through the stained glass into the chapel interior and even into the garden and out onto the street. Large patterns formed by metal and glass bands on the exterior of the building help to project the church's message out into the greater neighborhood—the shapes form huge crosses when seen from a distance.

PRECEDING PAGES: Viewed from the street, the chapel becomes a beacon of faith. **ABOVE:** Main level plan. **OPPOSITE:** The chapel, made of a mosaic of clear, translucent, and colored glass, exudes a warm interior glow in contrast to the busy urban streetscape outside.

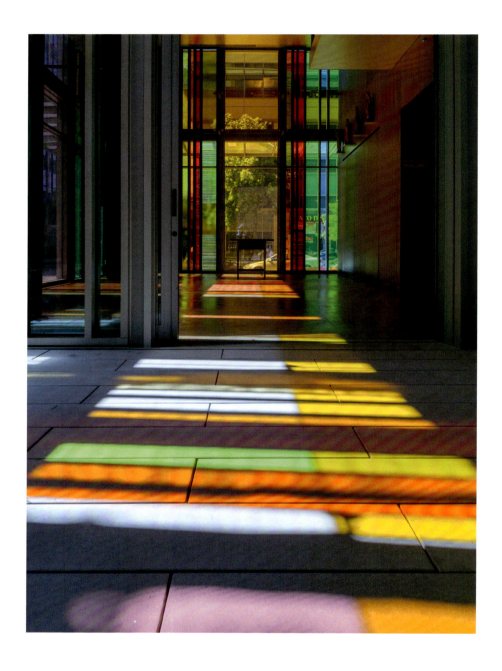

PRECEDING PAGES: The garden and chapel open to become one space.
ABOVE: Projected colored light creates a visual "procession" from the garden to
the simple altar inside. **OPPOSITE:** Projected patterns add another dimension
to the chapel. **OVERLEAF, LEFT:** Meditation garden located next to the chapel.

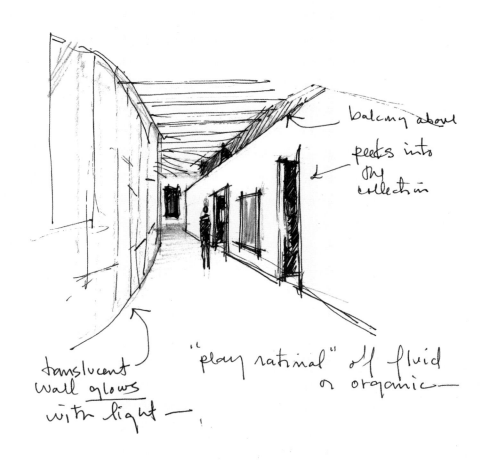

balcony above
peeks into
the
collection

translucent
wall glows
with light —,

"play rational" of fluid
or organic —

WORKING WITH LIGHT

I grew up in a region where the light is softened and refined by a constantly changing atmosphere, and is often muted by mist and clouds. I've noticed the mysterious, almost transcendent quality of light through these clouds, and the dramatic moments that result from pure sunlight beaming through a break in them. I've also noticed how water reflects light—with the sea being the largest, ever-present body of water in the region—and how this visual movement on the water brings the whole environment to life. The surface of the water sparkles with sunlight, and reflected light dances on the ceilings and walls of our homes.

In designing with light, I like to use it to create a variety of moods. Indirect light seems to generate a spiritual quality. Artist James Turrell has spent a lifetime exploring transcendent light in his skyspaces and light tunnels, and I've learned a tremendous amount from observing his work. Light can also be projected through translucent glass to create a softly illuminated, tranquil atmosphere. Light beamed through colored glass can project colors onto wall surfaces, creating ephemeral "paintings" of colored light; light reflected off colored surfaces gives a similar effect. The many ways to sculpt with light, and balance it within a space, allow us to play with illusions of infinity.

From a practical perspective, I have a number of preferences in working with light to create spaces for living. In my architecture, the flow between inside and outside space is important, and lighting design plays an essential part in this. At night, outside lighting needs to be strong enough to visually balance the indoor lighting. My preference at night is for strong light outside and soft light inside, which seems to make the indoor/outdoor spatial flow more coherent.

It's possible to balance light in a room by bringing in daylight from more than one source. This helps to avoid too much uncomfortable glare from one side, and create a more even illumination. Light can be bounced onto ceilings—off of which it then reflects—by using ledges or soffits at windows as "light shelves." This is an effective way to naturally illuminate interior spaces with pleasant, indirect light. The aim is to use just enough light, but not too much.

The mood of an environment is greatly affected by the quality of light. Bright light works well for larger, open, active spaces. On the other hand, you can use soft, ambient light to create a cozier, more intimate mood. Think of how firelight or candlelight creates the perfect romantic setting. My desire is always to use light to create a soft and warm ambience—for example,

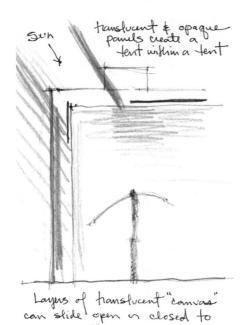

Sun

translucent & opaque panels create a tent within a tent

Layers of translucent "canvas" can slide open or closed to provide the appropriate level of light for each exhibit

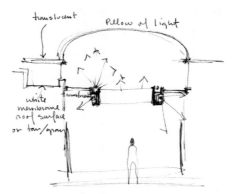

translucent

Pillow of light

white membrane roof surface or tan/gray

The light beams should do what the light wands do at my apartment it's so simple — put the light source in the middle & get even light all around —

The beams shouldn't look just like structural beams BUT more like wooden fins or struts — w/ some metal on them — They should look tech" — but incorporate natural wood —

by softening natural light through grilles, trellises, or translucent materials, and by using reflected light instead of direct sunlight.

Focused light can be used in a variety of ways to create more dramatic—sometimes even poetic—effects. This type of light can accentuate an art piece, or even elements of the architecture itself. You can flatter the people within a space by using light sources that make the most of their facial features, but avoid anything too direct or harsh. At the dining table, for example, light the table itself and let reflected light from its surface illuminate peoples' features. However, I also believe that a certain degree of contrast in the light makes people look good, wherever they are in the house.

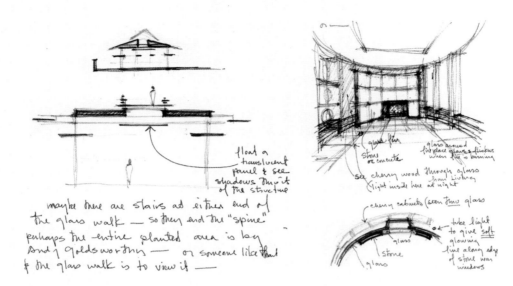

I always consider practicality when arranging everyday lighting—and little things can mean a lot. For instance, when writing or sketching, as a right-hander I always put the light source on my left to prevent forming shadows on the page when I write. Practical details like this are especially important in task lighting, and in areas such as kitchens or bathrooms, for example.

Ultimately, the relationship of the Earth to the sun defines who we are and how we perceive our whole environment. The rhythms of time are defined by Earth's orbit around the sun, and light from the sun warms us and illuminates our world. Our sight evolved in response to the presence of this light. Thus, we are creatures of light, but also of shadow. Light describes and delineates space through shade. And moving light—filtered through leaves in the breeze, or sparkling off the surface of the sea, shaped through the day by architectural elements—animates that space. As an architect, working with light is an opportunity to sculpt and modulate an element essential to our humanity.

PAGE 97: Sketch by Jim Olson of interior circulation space at the Lightcatcher, Whatcom Museum, Bellingham, Washington, 2007. **PRECEDING PAGE, LEFT:** Sketch by Olson of Jordan Schnitzer Museum of Art, Washington State University, Pullman, Washington, 2013. **PRECEDING PAGE, RIGHT:** Concept sketch by Olson for An American Place, Hunts Point, Washington, 2001. **ABOVE, LEFT:** Olson's sketch of the gallery at the House of Light, Medina, Washington, 2003. **ABOVE, RIGHT:** Olson's sketch of the living room at Glass Apartment, Seattle, Washington, 1999

COUNTRY GARDEN HOUSE

LOCATION: PORTLAND, OREGON, USA

COMPLETED: 2013

When two widowed people in their seventies get married, the big question is: "His house or hers?" The solution in this case was to live in his town, Portland, but to create a new house that would represent a new beginning for both of them. Both had collections of antiques and porcelain, and she had the idea of creating a barn-like structure with open spaces in which to display them.

This house is not my typical project, as it took me further into "traditional" architecture and interiors than I'm usually comfortable going, but I liked the clients and their vision. I also pursued my usual themes of vistas of art and nature, indoor/outdoor visual flow, use of natural materials, and the joining of landscape architecture, interiors, and art into a unified whole. I especially like some of the contrasts in the house—the rural feel on the suburban site; rough, rural, casual architecture against refined furniture and art/artifacts—it was a unique challenge, but with results that satisfied the clients ... and me.

Situated to be in harmony with its lush landscape, this home is built for a master gardener and takes every opportunity to draw in views of the surrounding gardens and rolling hills, while also creating a warm and comfortable space suitable for a multi-generational family. The form of the reclaimed barnwood-clad house is reminiscent of a farm structure or even a greenhouse, with its gridded glazing and pitched roof, and high windows at each end of the main volume flood the home with light. Gardens designed in collaboration with the client and notable plantsman Dan Hinkley are visible from every room, and window walls in the living area allow the gardens to become a part of the home. A green roof continues the home's emphasis on integrating into its natural surroundings.

The entry sequence brings visitors underneath leafy trellises to a front door that opens to a long vista through the living room, opening to views of the verdant hillside beyond. A long gallery corridor separates the private bedroom spaces from the more "public" living spaces, and showcases the owners' artworks. Their art extends into the main living areas with custom casework designed to display a rich collection of Asian porcelain, as well as a hand-painted mural by artist Leo Adams. Interior materials incorporate the earthy, textural feeling of the gardens, including cedar walls and reclaimed Baba fir floors that complement the owners' mix of antique and contemporary furnishings, including a coffee table that I designed. Exposed timber ceilings in the main volume lend a sense of rustic refinement that is complemented by the stone fireplace separating the den and living room. Easily accessible outdoor living spaces and ponds offer plentiful spaces for family gatherings woven into the lush surroundings.

PAGE 101: View of the house from the garden. **PRECEDING PAGES:** The hallway has a vista of nature at both ends. **ABOVE:** Site plan depicting house floor plan and gardens. **OPPOSITE, TOP:** The pitched roof of the home's main volume recalls vernacular barn and greenhouse architecture. **OPPOSITE, BOTTOM:** Throughout the home, window walls draw the lush garden foliage inside.

ABOVE, LEFT: The home's front door opens to a long vista through the living room with views of the verdant hillside beyond. **ABOVE, RIGHT:** Exposed timber ceilings in the main volume continue the barn-inspired character of the house.

CLIFF DWELLING

LOCATION: WHITE ROCK, BRITISH COLUMBIA, CANADA

COMPLETED: 2013

This house is situated on a long, thin site at the edge of a south-facing bluff above Semiahmoo Bay, between a road and railroad tracks. Its design creates privacy while also taking advantage of spectacular views of the water, islands, and mountains to the west, east, and south. I saw the house as presenting a sculptural opportunity, and worked hard on composition. The client liked my design for Northwoods House, while I was also inspired by the work of Canadian architect Arthur Erickson.

From the northern approach, the home is protected and unassuming. Thick concrete walls shield the occupants from the sight and sound of the busy road above, while glass window walls and expansive decks make the most of the views. Over three levels, the house slowly reveals its layers: principal living areas (living room, dining room, and kitchen) are collected on the main level just down from the formal entry gallery, on the west side. The master suite is private and tucked away on the second level on the east side, while the family room, children's bedrooms, sauna, and exercise area on the ground floor open out to the lap pool and spa outside.

In the northern climate, harvesting sunlight is important. The living room window wall captures the light and on warm days it can completely open up to the terrace, forming one space. The design hierarchy was to some extent intuitive, with the great power of the solid concrete wall behind opening up to a wide, sunlit space in front—like a cave or cliff dwelling; responding to the earth, meeting the sun.

The simple palette of materials is durable and low-maintenance. The client wanted an ultra-modern house with concrete as a key material, along with steel and glass. Concrete walls and floors and natural unfinished zinc siding are contrasted with warm Douglas fir ceilings and soffits. The cascading layers of the house are connected by a cast-in-place concrete stair, and glass guardrails are capped with a stainless-steel handrail. The stair opens to a gallery on each level with views out over the bay.

PRECEDING PAGES: South facade. OPPOSITE, TOP: The home is perched above a set of railroad tracks on the shores of Semiahmoo Bay. OPPOSITE, BOTTOM: In the living room, solid concrete walls anchor the home into the earth, while glass window walls capture the sunlight from the south.

OPPOSITE: A "magic window" creates a seamless connection between interior spaces and the trees, water, and islands beyond. **ABOVE:** Plan of top two levels. **OVERLEAF:** Reflections in the master bedroom windows reveal the view. **PAGE 116:** Concrete stairs connect all levels of the home.

NATURE

I grew up in America's Pacific Northwest, where the foliage is lush and nature is benevolent. As a kid, I spent almost all of my spare time outdoors—in the woods, by the river, or on the beaches of Puget Sound. In the Northwest, the trees are tall and nature is all-encompassing. As a result I feel part of nature, not separate from it. Its miracles have always fascinated and inspired me.

The way I see both life in general and architecture in particular is strongly influenced by the natural world. I look at the layering and variety of colors and textures in nature, and how each unique piece of anything affects the whole. For example, I observe how a curving madrone tree plays off the straight vertical line of a nearby fir tree. Their differences bring out the individual beauty in each. The line of the horizon over the water underscores and defines the shape and form of the mountain or island beyond. I observe how translucent objects such as paper-thin leaves or slivers of agate glow like precious jewels when the sun illuminates them from behind, or how a pale flower in a dark forest stands out so dramatically, making it easy for the bees and hummingbirds to seek it out. I see how the bark on driftwood or trees silvers and bleaches as it weathers, softening the material visually; how the rocks on the beach are a hundred different colors, yet as a whole, the beach appears to be a soft, warm gray— nature's version of pointillism. I see, too, how animal dens and nests illustrate the intuitive concepts of prospect/refuge—safe places in which to rest and raise families—protected, warm spaces from which they can see out, but from which they will not be seen.

One purpose of architecture is to help us observe the landscape around us. Architecture can intensify our amazement at the beauty of nature, while providing a place of refuge. The colors and materials of the landscape influence my architecture, and I like to weave my buildings into the natural landscape. I see the land, the trees, and the architecture as all part of the same environment, the same composition. Sometimes trees break up the facade and frame elements of the architecture from the inside, and they can also bring movement and life. Architecture and trees work together rather than against each other.

Water plays its part too, connecting vistas to the sky and adding vitality to a composition. Sometimes I use my architecture to frame an expanse of water. The ultimate water element is of course the ocean, with its own monumental power and its connection to the wider cosmos via its vast reflection.

I aim to facilitate a close relationship with nature through my architecture. As architects we can frame nature and thereby help people focus their attention on it. We can compose views of

foliage and landscape in the same way that we might compose art, framing it with our windows, beams, or columns. We can increase our sense of closeness to nature by hiding the edges of windows to create the illusion that there is no barrier between indoor space and the landscape outside. Ultimately, the landscape is to me about life: about simply being alive, but also about realizing that our whole planet is teeming with life. It is about appreciating the miracle we are all a part of. We are part of nature and our dwellings are part of the landscape as much as a bird's nest or a beehive—everything is connected. One of the greatest luxuries we have is to choose to live close to nature. Just stand quietly in the woods and simply look and listen—you will understand that the forest is teeming with life, and you will feel the connectedness of all things. Creating a relationship or connection with the land helps us understand who we are. My hope is that, by bringing people closer to nature with my architecture, they will learn to love it too. The more we love and appreciate nature, the more we will feel compelled to protect it.

PRECEDING PAGE: Sketch of Mount Rainier by Jim Olson from 2008. **ABOVE:** Section of living room overlooking nature at Longbranch Cabin, Longbranch, Washington. Sketch from 1998.

March 4, 2012 Maunakea room 4PM
sunny & warm ——
   worked on elevations of new bedroom
etc. —— & like it now ——
   the idea of flower in the forest
works well —— here's a conceptual
sketch

New bedroom as
seen from field
a flower in the forest

ABOVE: Sketch by Olson of master bedroom wing at Longbranch Cabin from 2012.

BELLEVUE BOTANICAL GARDEN VISITOR CENTER

LOCATION: BELLEVUE, WASHINGTON, USA

COMPLETED: 2014

Since opening in 1992, the 53-acre (21-hectare) Bellevue Botanical Garden has become one of the most popular public gardens in the Pacific Northwest. A growing interest in native planting and gardening, as well as expanded programs, has drawn large crowds. Balancing civic function with residential scale and attention to detail, the design of the new visitor center creates intimate, inspirational spaces that allow for exploration and quiet reflection. The scope of the project, which is targeting LEED® Gold certification, included new construction, renovation and site work. The centerpiece is a new 8,500-square-foot (710 sq m) visitor center complex, which includes a covered outdoor orientation space, gift shop, meeting space, concession area, education space, office space, and restrooms. The areas are arranged in a series of smaller structures situated under two large, organizing roofs; together, they read as a unified L-shaped building.

The project also includes the renovation of the Shorts Residence (built in 1957), designed by noted Northwest architect Paul Kirk, one of my heroes as a young architect. The 2,300-square-foot (214 sq m) former residence of Cal and Harriet Shorts, which has served as the visitor center for the gardens since its inception, now functions as an auxiliary library and living room for the garden. Our team included landscape architects Swift Company and renowned plantsman Dan Hinkley, who were dedicated to bringing out the potential of these gardens.

I was drawn to the project because I am especially interested in the interplay of nature and architecture. Just as in a museum or an art collector's home, the architecture is deferential, providing a frame for viewing objects in a focused way—only here it is plants instead of art. Kirk's simple, linear architecture inspired the new buildings we created. It acts as a counterpoint as well as a frame to the organic flora of the garden. In terms of layout, the gardens were charming but seemed to lack order, and wayfinding was difficult. Our new layout, like the buildings themselves, brought structure to the organic arrangement of the garden and made the grounds easier to navigate. Sustainability was a priority in both buildings and gardens.

Courtyards interspersed between the structures reinforce connections to landscape, while broad roof overhangs, fernery walls, and gardens unite the spaces and create a natural flow between indoors and out. The educational component is one large space that can be subdivided into several classrooms and meeting spaces; these spaces can expand via large rolling doors that open onto the gardens.

PAGE 121: Rational architecture frames abstract nature. **PRECEDING PAGES:** The main entrance leads to a vista of the gardens. Visitors' experience is grounded in nature from the moment they enter the site. **ABOVE:** Visitor center floor plan. **OPPOSITE, TOP:** Interior educational spaces can expand via large rolling doors that open onto the gardens. These flexible spaces can accommodate a range of educational uses. **OPPOSITE, BOTTOM:** This outdoor "promenade" connects all the building's rooms together.

PRECEDING PAGES: Outdoor education area where students and tour groups receive orientation to the gardens. **ABOVE:** New buildings bring order to the visitor flow, delineating clear pathways to the gardens.

LONGBRANCH CABIN

LOCATION: LONGBRANCH, WASHINGTON, USA

COMPLETED: 1959, 1981, 1997, 2003, 2014

In 1912, my grandparents built a summer cottage on a forested site on Puget Sound, and I spent summers and many weekends there as a child. When I was a first-year architecture student, my dad gave me five hundred dollars and said, "Go build a bunkhouse": my first great opportunity. Nestled amidst the trees of this waterside forest and raised on stilts, the tiny cabin I built sat respectfully on the landscape. When my grandparents' cottage was destroyed by fire in the 1960s, the bunkhouse was all that was left on the property.

What began as a 200-square-foot (19 sq m) bunkhouse in 1959 has seen the addition of several interconnected rooms through a series of remodelings in 1981, 1997, 2003, and 2014. Each successive expansion has reused and integrated the previous structure rather than erasing it, revealing the process of the architecture's evolution.

In the 1980s, the retreat consisted of three tiny pavilions linked by wooden platforms. In 2003, the pavilions were connected by a unifying roof, creating a single form grounded onto the hillside and projecting out over the landscape. The living room's large wall of glass frames a view of the adjoining grassy field and Puget Sound, visually blending indoors and outdoors. In 2014, a master bedroom and two guest rooms were added. I wanted the bedroom to stand out, and my wife Katherine loves to read, so I created a library that also works as circulation. We wanted a sense of refuge so I created a small enclosed private courtyard and surrounded the bed with solid wood walls. I experimented with more random patterns, and created a vista looking out into the beautiful woods, ending with a three-dimensional "magic window."

The cabin is intentionally subdued in color and texture, allowing it to recede into the woods and defer to the beauty of the landscape. Materials enhance this natural connection, reflecting the silvery hues of the overcast Northwest sky and tying the building to the forest floor. Simple, readily available materials were used throughout: wood-framed walls are sheathed in plywood or recycled boards, inside and outside; doubled pairs of steel columns support beams that in turn support exposed roof structures. Interior spaces appear to flow seamlessly to the outside as materials continue from inside to out through invisible sheets of glass.

The cabin has been a work in progress since it began, with each transformation acknowledging our changing priorities: first a bunkhouse for friends, then an experimental weekend retreat for a young couple and family, and now, a quiet place for contemplation and creative work, and a comfortable place for visiting grandchildren, extended family, and friends.

PRECEDING PAGES: The building has woven itself into the forest over fifty-eight years. OPPOSITE: The master bedroom deck cantilevers into the trees, creating a "squirrel's-eye" view. OVERLEAF: The transparent library allows a view of trees and water from the enclosed courtyard.

ABOVE: Main floor plan and site. **OPPOSITE:** The house is placed in the trees at the north edge of the field, where it is warmed by south sun. The field is left open as the main "outdoor room" on the site.

ABOVE: At the end of the library hall is a "magic" bay window that creates the illusion of being outside. **OPPOSITE:** Bookshelves lining the library hall frame the vista into the woods at the end.

ABOVE: The "magic window" and trees work together to frame the water view from the living room. **OPPOSITE:** Colors and materials visually connect the woods and beach to the interior. **OVERLEAF:** Exterior view of master bedroom with deck extending into the forest. The deck offers an opportunity to be with the squirrels high in the trees.

OPPOSITE: The master bedroom walls are clad with natural spruce boards cut in
random widths, some rough and some smooth. Some of the smooth boards are coated
with clear lacquer to reflect light. ABOVE: View from the master bedroom to the beach,
looking across Puget Sound. OVERLEAF: The master bedroom from the deck.
The library is to the right.

BLAKELY ISLAND
ART STUDIO

LOCATION: BLAKELY ISLAND, WASHINGTON, USA

COMPLETED: 2014

I've worked for these clients for many years—they were among my very first, and I've known them since childhood. Over the years I've remodeled their house, and designed a condominium and an island retreat for them, which is the site of this project. The main house was built in the 1980s, then later a separate cottage was added as the master bedroom, and then a combined guesthouse/garage.

An intimate study in scale, this latest addition of a compact art studio makes the most of its remote site on a forested bluff overlooking the water in the San Juan Islands. Consisting essentially of a single room, the wood-framed cabin offers flexible space as either a painting studio or a guesthouse. As the couple aged they found they spent more time at their retreat, and the wife wanted a place to make her watercolor paintings. She chose a spot where you could look down into the water, as if you were suspended in the air. I thought of the original retreat building like a bird on a cliff about to take flight— the window overlooking the water was a triangle, like a beak. This new studio became, in my mind, the "child" of the "mother bird" just up the hill—at one with the sky.

The back of the structure gently nestles into the hillside, bounded by existing trees and boulders, enclosing a micro kitchen and bathroom. The front cantilevers out over the slope, its open studio space circumscribed on three sides by floor-to-ceiling glass walls. The front wall breaks the square with a triangular bay window that angles out to a point, opening the cabin up to sweeping views of the water and islands beyond, creating an inspiring spot to set up an easel.

Though the interior space is minimal, the design merges the cabin into its forested site with doors opening to decks extending off either side, allowing the modest quarters to feel more expansive. Clere-story windows enhance the high ceiling and give the sloped roof the appearance of floating. These windows also allow additional light to flood the cabin, adding to a feeling of openness. A low interior wall delineates the studio area from the kitchen and bathroom, while also providing storage space and shelving. Ultimately, when standing in this cabin, the awareness is not of the interior spaces, but instead of the surrounding trees and the expansive seascape below.

ABSTRACTION

As a kid, I loved to draw and wanted to become an artist. My dad often told me if I could make a career out of what I liked to do as a hobby, I would always be happy. I also liked to build things, so my career choice evolved into architecture. As an architect, I've taken my love of art along with me—I see my architecture through the eyes of an artist. The way I think is more along the lines of a painter or a weaver than a sculptor.

I've spent my career incorporating art into my architecture. I often design for art collectors and I try to let the sensibility of their collection lead me to an appropriate architectural expression. I love collaborating with artists—their way of thinking about a project is very inspiring. They add a layer of richness to the environment that cannot be achieved through architecture alone. I see art as an important expression of human creativity, and this is what I believe will take us to the next level in our evolution as a species; we need to keep this creative spark alive if we are to survive and succeed in the future.

When I'm starting a project I sometimes go to an art museum and just wander around looking. Ideas come to me there, and sparks ignite in my brain. I like all kinds of art, and it interests me on many levels. I've worked with historical collections such as Spanish Colonial and Pre-Columbian art, and I've also worked with many modern and contemporary art pieces. The historical art I'm most drawn to is ancient Egyptian—the sensibility fits my own. I'm attracted to the primal, abstract shapes and patterns found in the work of some South American and Mexican modern artists. I'm also drawn to modern masters like Mark Rothko and Donald Judd for their purity, simplicity, and treatment of proportion. My favorite artist of our time is James Turrell: his work is transcendent.

When I experience art that I truly love it is delicious to me. It is like a drink of cold water when you are parched—it is thrilling and satisfying to the soul. Intuition plays a key role in art because aesthetics are subjective—they come from the gut. And yet, there are also tangible reasons why we are drawn to one thing more than another. Composition and proportions play a vital role in making this elusive thing called beauty. Even an abstract art piece can tell a story and add layers of depth and richness to everyday life. Art can make me see something in a new way—perhaps in a way I'd never imagined before.

In the 1970s I began doing transcendental meditation, and since then—for the past forty years—I've meditated twice a day for twenty minutes each day. It was in the early 1980s that I first became familiar with the work of James Turrell and assisted him with an exhibition of his work

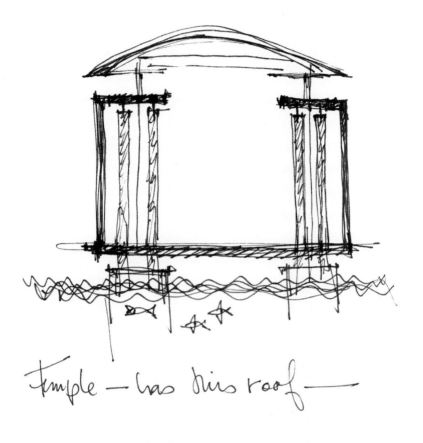

Temple — has this roof —

in Seattle. When I look into some of Turrell's light works, I see something similar to what I perceive in my own mind while meditating: a dissolving of the material world and an awareness of something beyond it, a kind of serene abstraction. Over the years I've tried to bring glimpses of this serene abstraction—that "beyond"—into people's lives through my architecture.

I've achieved this in various ways, through a range of architectural devices. The "infinite ceiling," for example, is directly inspired by the work of Turrell—in projects such as Garden House, Zen House, and Hudson Valley Residence, there are rooms where I created a "dome" and details visually dissolve into a hazy suggestion of endless mist. The reflective quality of glass can create ghostly layered images. Water reflects the sky and becomes a magic medium. It is often moving and shifting, so it becomes "alive" and brings an abstract vitality to our environment, while light reflecting off that moving water dances on walls and ceilings, bringing them to life as well. The ocean is the ultimate body of water because it is so vast and reflects the infinite sky—I've tried to frame the

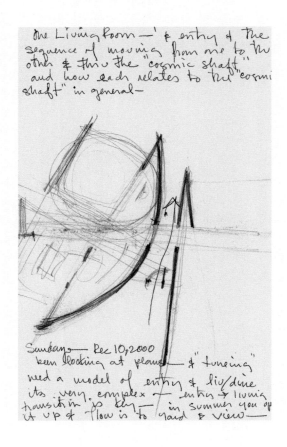

ocean to focus on its transcendent quality, especially at the horizon, where earth meets sky.

Framing views of sky and water enables us to contemplate the fact that some things in existence

endure forever, while the poetry of passing clouds accentuates the fleeting quality of the present.

A further method I have found of expressing transcendence is to defy gravity, to make elements

seem to be floating in space. I sometimes try to hide the support of a long cantilevered roof so that

the roof plane appears suspended in space, like a bird with outstretched wings, taking flight.

PAGE 153: Watercolor by Olson of entrance to An American Place, Hunts Point, Washington, 2000.
PRECEDING PAGE: Olson sketch of the living room of Garden House, Atherton, California, 1995.
ABOVE: Plan study by Olson of Lake House, Mercer Island, Washington, sketch done in 2000.

HAVEN OF REFLECTION

LOCATION: SEATTLE, WASHINGTON, USA

COMPLETED: 2014

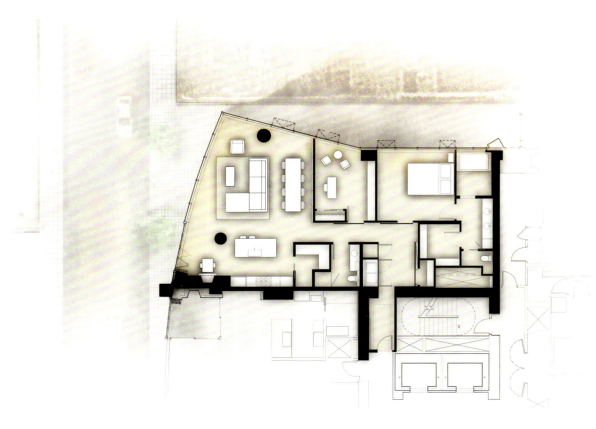

We originally designed a house for this client and her husband, now deceased, in the 1990s. She loves to travel so she moved to a small condominium in downtown Seattle with a spectacular view of the city, Puget Sound, and the Olympic Mountains beyond, but the original interior didn't do justice to the 23rd-floor unit's sweeping views of Elliott Bay. A significant structural renovation and complete overhaul of the finishes and furnishings fulfill the owner's request for a spare but warm and welcoming living space that celebrates the view of the bay beyond.

The apartment had the problem of a circuitous, unappealing route from the front door to the living room and its spectacular views. It featured stark track lighting and a sight line that led directly into the master bedroom. The unit's main entryway is now softened with an uplit ceiling alcove, replacing the track lighting. I decided to make the journey down the narrow hallway into a beautiful adventure by lining the walls with sliding wooden *shoji* screens that conceal entrances to various rooms and utilities. The concept is rather like moving through a Japanese garden, giving a sense of anticipation.

The main view room was all window on one side and a solid wall at the back—it was a small room that housed the living, dining, and kitchen areas. We created a reflective wall on the back instead, to give a sense of space and also to reflect the amazing view on the other side. Rather than make the reflective wall entirely of plain mirrors, I wanted a subtler expression that went into the realm of arts and crafts, so we layered sheets of glass over sheets of stainless steel that had been blowtorched, turning them toasty brownish. I also designed most of the furniture to unify the environment.

An existing glazed atrium afforded quasi-outdoor seating, yet interrupted the panoramic view from the living area and severely crowded the kitchen. By removing the glass surround and shifting the color scheme of the finishes, the reclaimed space gracefully incorporates the similarly redesigned living area and also allows for additional workspace in the kitchen. A custom-built dining table can be used for two or to seat a large dinner party. With the use of stacked metal and glass trays, flowers, and art, the table can become an artistic display, leaving one end for intimate dining.

PAGE 157: Reflections of Puget Sound. **PRECEDING PAGES:** Main living area with Puget Sound on left and reflective wall to the right. **ABOVE:** Floor plan. **OPPOSITE, TOP:** At the back of the main living area, a glass wall layered over torched stainless-steel panels reflects the atmospheric light of nearby Elliott Bay. **OPPOSITE, BOTTOM:** Sliding wood screens throughout the main hallway open to reveal bedrooms and utilities. **OVERLEAF:** Furniture designed by Jim Olson.

HONG KONG
TOY COMPANY

LOCATION: HONG KONG, CHINA

COMPLETED: 2010, 2014

Two projects encompassed complete remodeling of the offices, lobby, toy showroom, and conference rooms for the Hong Kong headquarters of a toy company in two sequential locations. In 2010 we designed the original location on the sixth floor of an office tower in Tsim Sha Tsui. In 2014 the company moved to a new location four and a half miles (7 km) east, and we designed this, too. The design goals for the projects included increasing the amount of natural light throughout the offices, and emphasizing the company's products and their display.

In the original location, previously covered and mirrored windows were replaced and transformed through the addition of a translucent glass layer inserted inside the exterior glazing. The result was a softly glowing interior light that brightened the office spaces and naturally illuminated toy displays. In the company's new location on the top two floors of the Elite Center building in Kwun Tong, shown on these two pages, a red resin wall behind the reception desk greets visitors before they ascend up a steel staircase to the second floor, which houses showrooms and meeting areas. Here, double-sided display cases maximize viewing space for changing products from the company's ever-evolving toy line.

In both locations, a naturally inspired material palette creates a quiet backdrop for the company's bright and lively toys, including cedar ceilings, locally sourced stone and neutral-toned fabrics. Teak and ash were selected for featured furnishings, including entry benches and the CEO's work table. Materials were also selected for their ability to withstand the high humidity and warm climate of Hong Kong. The showroom features a series of acid-etched glass walls and shelving that highlights the brightly colored toys displayed there without overpowering them.

We also designed a sculpture based on one of the company's toy foam rockets, and photographer Marsha Burns was commissioned to create portraits of some of the company's vintage toys to hang in the lobby.

PRECEDING PAGES: Guests are greeted at the main lobby in the company's new location. **OPPOSITE:** A steel and glass staircase winds around a glowing red resin accent wall behind the reception desk. Photographs by artist Marsha Burns of historic toys line the perimeter walls.

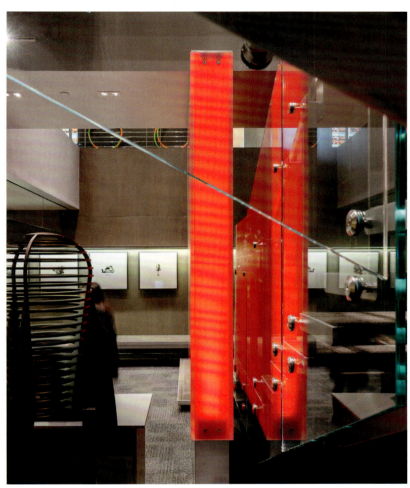

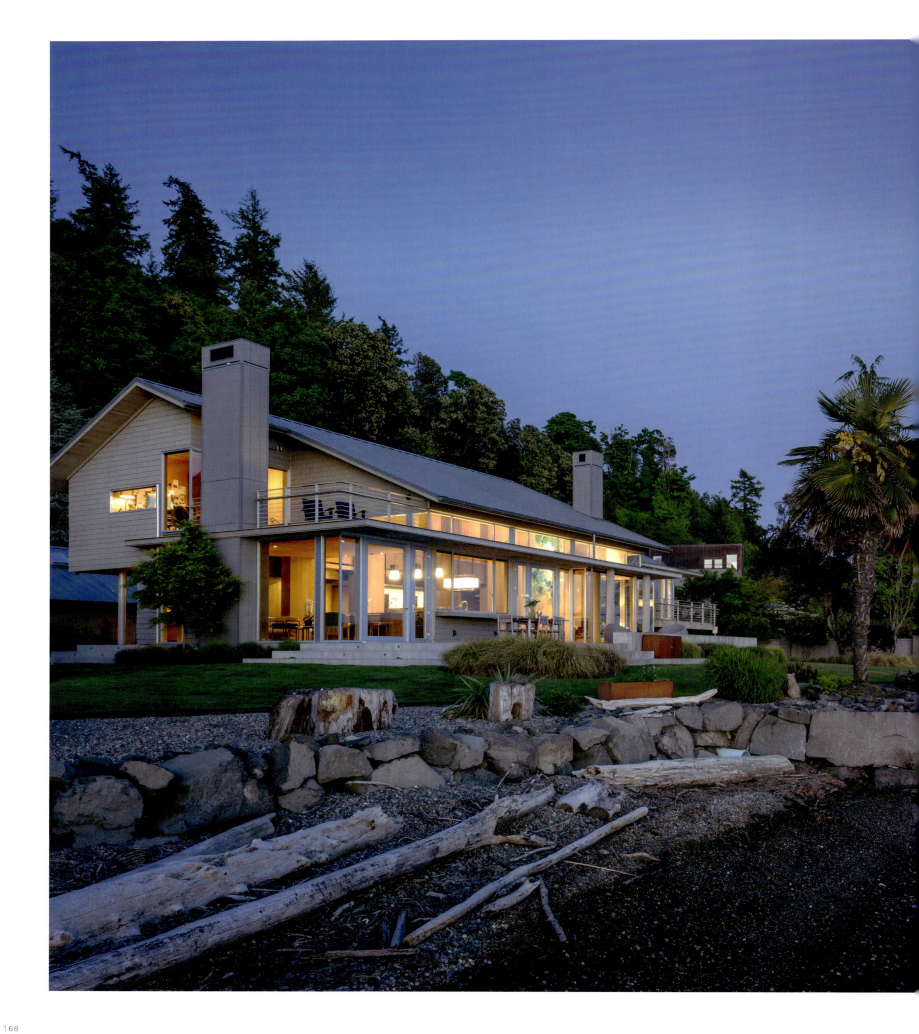

FOX ISLAND
RESIDENCE

LOCATION: FOX ISLAND, WASHINGTON, USA

COMPLETED: 2014

This is a remodeling of a family home that an architect friend, Dan Calvin, designed for the clients in the 1970s. The Fox Island beachfront residence has unobstructed views of Puget Sound and an island wildlife area to the west. Opening up these previously constrained views and integrating the family's active coastal lifestyle into the home served as the primary directives for the new design. It's a special opportunity to remodel a house that the clients have lived in for many years. They know the site so well: the best views, the direction of winds, and how the sun interacts with the site throughout the year.

When the project first came into our firm, one of my partners, Scott Allen, was the lead designer. Scott left the firm to start his own practice, and the client asked that I take over the design lead, while project manager William Franklin stayed on the project. What, therefore, were my contributions to the project? There were big things like the general driftwood color palette, which ties the house visually to the beach, as well as the addition of silver metals like zinc, aluminum, nickel, and stainless steel that blend with the driftwood but also sparkle. We pushed for all wood on floors, walls, ceilings, and cabinets in the main two-story space—and all this wood warms up the living area visually and softens the acoustics. The detailed metalwork inside and out adds a crisp counterpoint to the wood surfaces.

An elevated roofline and a new row of clerestory windows on the home's water-facing side, along with wall-height windows replacing the original truncated glazing, brighten a previously darker and more compressed living area. Hidden pivot points in several of these window walls open the west side of the home to the outdoors, extending the livable area out to the newly remodeled deck.

Inside, exposed wood pillars supporting the clerestory windows are paired with a corresponding row of pillars on the exterior, creating a visual link to the outdoors. Beach grasses push up to the wall-height windows in the main living area, further connecting the interior to the exterior. Reclaimed antique wood floors, sandy-colored cedar board ceilings and interior walls, and nickel and cold-rolled steel fireplaces continue the Northwest natural aesthetic inside.

The interior offers a neutral backdrop for the client's eclectic art collection. Large, colorful wall-mounted glass pieces by artist Dale Chihuly find new life in the subdued interior. Opening up the stairwell and upper-level hallway created new views of the artworks installed below, generating a visual connection between the home's two floors, and to the coastal landscape beyond.

PRECEDING PAGES: Interior space spills out onto the deck, lawn, and water below. **ABOVE:** Main level plan. **OPPOSITE:** In the main living area, a nickel and cold-rolled steel fireplace reflects the silvery hues of the coastal landscape and complements the wood surfaces.

ABOVE: Reclaimed Baba wood floors, cedar walls and ceilings, white oak custom cabinetry, and a walnut table lend warmth and informality to the beach house. **OPPOSITE:** The open upper-level hallway adds to the sense of transparency at the entrance.

CITY CABIN

LOCATION: SEATTLE, WASHINGTON, USA

COMPLETED: 2015

The client for this project, in one of Seattle's most established and dense residential areas, is a close friend whom I have known for over fifty years. She is a free spirit whose father was an architect, so she understands the design process. She is also a neighbor at Longbranch and loved my cabin, so it became the inspiration and model for her new "city" house. We spent many summer afternoons at our picnic table at Longbranch designing her "cabin in the city."

She wanted a private urban refuge that would connect her to nature, so we sited the house on the northwest corner of an ordinary city lot to maximize the garden areas on the south and east sides and surrounded it with trees; landscape artist Brandon Peterson designed the planting on the site. Organized into two wings, with the bedrooms, storage, laundry, and pantry areas extending in opposite directions off a central gathering space, the house has a staggered footprint and glazing that increases sun exposure and garden views. The heart of the home, in plan and function, is a single volume defined by a 16-foot-high (4.9 m) ceiling and full-height window-wall overlooking the gardens to the southeast, reinforcing the visual connection to the "urban wilderness." Clerestory windows maximize solar gains and impart lightness while maintaining privacy.

The airy central space is also ideal for the client's fine collection of Native American art, whose culture prizes sustainable living, values echoed in the client's passionate environmentalism. The color palette of the interior finishes draws inspiration from the art. Concrete floors are waxed and tinted with a custom red hue, and walls and ceilings are made from A/C-grade plywood chosen for its durability and simplicity. On the exterior, old-growth fir siding reclaimed from a fruit storage warehouse will weather naturally with minimal maintenance, and durable galvanized steel roofing, downspouts and beam endcaps complement the wood finishes and will patina with time. Ultimately, the house is designed to be "net zero"—it produces as much energy as it uses—so the house's sustainable materials are enhanced by super-efficient windows from Germany, photovoltaic panels, a green roof, and an air-to-water heat pump.

PRECEDING PAGES: View of the home from the enclosed garden. OPPOSITE, TOP: Although the home is located on a small urban lot, the dense garden creates a sense of privacy and wilderness. OPPOSITE, BOTTOM: Exterior materials, such as reclaimed old-growth fir siding and galvanized steel roofing, will weather over time.

ABOVE: The design incorporates niches and displays throughout for the client's extensive collection of Native American art. Kitchen, dining, and living are all one space. **OPPOSITE:** South-facing window walls in the main living area make the garden part of the house and maximize solar heating.

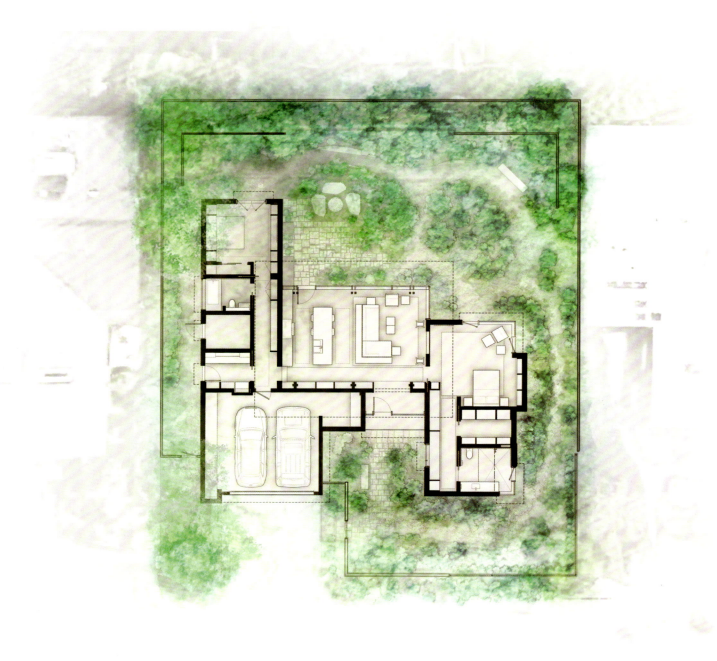

ABOVE: Floor plan and site plan. **OPPOSITE:** Outdoor gathering places, interwoven with the home's gardens, make the site feel like a natural refuge.

FOSS WATERWAY SEAPORT

LOCATION: TACOMA, WASHINGTON, USA

COMPLETED: 2015

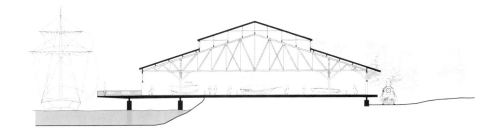

The Foss Waterway Seaport, a maritime museum, occupies the last remaining section of Balfour Dock—a heavy timber-frame warehouse that was nearly a mile long, and defined Tacoma's waterfront for almost a century. Built in 1900, the remaining 350-foot-long (107 m) portion straddles the shoreline immediately beneath Tacoma's downtown. Originally designed and constructed in the bridge-building language of nineteenth-century railroad engineering, this remaining portion now supports the largest maritime heritage and education center on the West Coast.

A friend on the board of the Maritime Museum took me to see the site in the hope that I could help them prepare the building for the future. As soon as I entered I was astounded by the strength of the wooden structure and the monumentality of the space. It was raw and gutsy, and I had the same kind of feeling as when I first visited Louis Kahn's Salk Institute in California. I saw my goal as presenting the power of that historic structure, not only beautiful in its shape and proportions, but with a monumental scale and a visceral power similar to grand ancient structures such as Egyptian temples.

There had been a crumbling brick wall at the north of the building where the entrance was, but we were given permission to replace this with the key feature of a new glazed north facade, revealing the 150-foot-long (46 m) historic trusses from the exterior as you approach the museum. This glazed facade acts as a beacon, connecting passing visitors with the site's past by revealing the historic architecture and the activities within. The new 40,000-square-foot (3,716 sq m) public facility now features indoor program spaces, docks and floats for recreational and educational boating, and public open spaces for events, festivals, and casual activities. The improvements make the Seaport the centerpiece of the adaptive reuse and rehabilitation project.

PRECEDING PAGES: A new glazed north facade reveals the 150-foot-long (46 m) historic trusses within. **ABOVE:** Section looking south. **OPPOSITE:** The building's waterfront site recalls the historic shipping industry.

JW MARRIOTT LOS CABOS
BEACH RESORT AND SPA

LOCATION: PUERTO LOS CABOS, BAJA, MEXICO

COMPLETED: 2015

When the client asked me to design a hotel in Baja, Mexico, on a site with a powerful desert landscape and an endless panorama of the Pacific Ocean, I said, "I'd love to but I've never done a hotel before." To which he replied, "I've seen your work, and if you can design those houses, you can design my hotel." These words marked the beginning of a great collaboration and friendship.

To me, the ocean, with its soft blue color and vast horizon, is a deeply spiritual place. The key goal of the design was to create intimate connections with the ocean from a variety of places within the complex. Because the resort is 35 feet (11 m) above the ocean, one objective was to provide visitors with a view framing the horizon from the main arrival hall, which appears to draw the water into the resort. Just past the main entry, two infinity pools appear to connect with the water beyond. And as visitors explore intuitive pathways throughout the 299-room property, ocean views, native landscaping, and sculpted sand dunes provide unexpected views and experiences from nearly every vantage point.

The drama of the site is desert meeting ocean—opposites attract. We wanted to express the contrasts between sand and water: Smooth concrete and stucco, whose color was derived from the surrounding desert, are used throughout the complex and designed to appear native to the site. Open travertine-covered hallways and floors, combined with local soil aggregates, further blend the physical boundaries of indoors and outdoors, site and architecture.

The site, set on a hill with mountains behind and facing south overlooking water, exhibited perfect feng shui. The resort's scale is vast, but we designed small, cozy places inside and out to create a sense of intimacy, like a small city or a village. Honing the grandeur of sprawling resort to a human scale starts at the entry hall, where a cadence of columns inspired by the order and scale of pre-Columbian monumental architecture draws visitors forward. In the grand public spaces, such as the 8,000-square-foot (743 sq m) ballroom, large steel girders are wrapped in dark wood, and soffits lend warmth and reduced scale to large spaces. The guest rooms, library, bar, and restaurant incorporate rich textures and warm desert tones that lend a soft earthy elegance to interior spaces. Art pieces commissioned from artists including Jaume Plensa, Jorge Yázpik, and Sam Falls are set throughout the interior and exterior spaces, and in some guest rooms.

Reinforcing its connection to the surroundings, the landscape design weaves together indigenous species, including the Cardon plant, a type of thorn scrub, and native torote and palo blanco trees. The verticality of royal, date, and Mexican fan palms ease the transition between built and natural forms, while exotic plants provide bolder colors in the sunken gardens, such as the Gardens of Paradise.

When I'm there, I really enjoy just sitting and watching people move about the resort, it feels like a small town. We tried to create a place that was genuine and natural—landscape, buildings, interiors, and furnishings that come together in a unified design that feels at home in this striking environment. I'm always surprised that this large-scale resort is really just like my houses, but bigger. The trust and support of our client was key.

PRECEDING PAGES: The simple order of the architecture reinforces the calm of the ocean. OPPOSITE, TOP: The hotel's main entrance is bounded by a garden of native plants surrounding the auto court. Visitors enter around the onyx wall. OPPOSITE, BOTTOM: After passing by the onyx wall, the hotel's architecture creates an immediate visual connection to the ocean by framing the blue horizon.

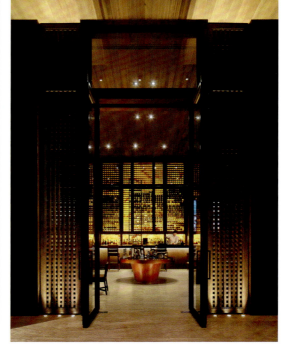

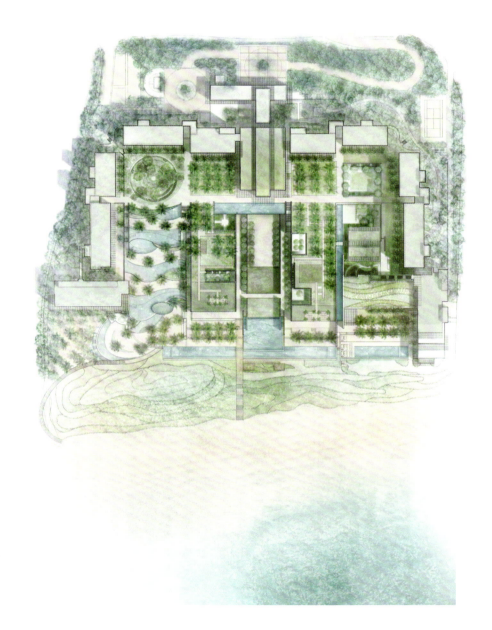

OPPOSITE, TOP: In the entry hallway,
the cadence of the monumental columns
draws visitors toward the ocean beyond.
OPPOSITE, BOTTOM: On the sides of
the lobby and overlooking the ocean, the
rich textures and tones of the library and bar
establish an earthy elegance often found in
historic Mexican haciendas. TOP: Section
through lobby. ABOVE: Site plan.

BELOW AND OPPOSITE: A series of infinity-edge pools throughout the property connects the resort to the ocean below. The stone sculpture is by Mexico City artist, Jorge Yázpik.

ABOVE, LEFT: Exterior walkways formed of travertine, stucco, and concrete take inspiration from the nearby dunes in their subdued, sandy palette. **OPPOSITE, RIGHT:** Throughout, framed views of sea and sky merge with swimming pools that appear to draw the ocean into the resort.

BELOW: The walkway to the hotel's Jasha Spa bridges a pair of mosaic-tiled vitality pools.
OPPOSITE: Custom-commissioned artworks like Jaume Plensa's Soul XII punctuate the resort's expansive grounds. **OVERLEAF:** The architecture's order can make an everyday moment feel like a sacred ceremony.

ABOVE AND OPPOSITE: Trellised outdoor terraces throughout the hotel offer sheltered respite from the sun.
OVERLEAF: At the end of the entrance colonnade, the horizon line expands. Terraces off the bar to the right,
library to the left. **PAGE 204:** The mood of the water is constantly changing, and reflecting pools visually
bring the ocean right up to the lobby.

INFLUENCES

I've never sought to capture a particular moment or movement in my architecture. I don't read the architectural press much, and I'm not what I'd call "hip" in my architecture. My inspirations come from buildings and architects across time, from the temples of ancient Egypt to the mentors I've had closer to home.

In Egypt, what inspires me is the massiveness, the elemental quality, and the proportions. I treasure the traditional architecture of Japan for its sensitive relationship with nature, exquisite detailing, and experiential and sequential approach. In the buildings of the Italian Renaissance, it is the integration of landscape, architecture, and art that inspires me.

Then there are the great works of modernism—buildings like Le Corbusier's Villa Savoye, La Tourette, Ronchamp. I am moved by Mies van der Rohe's Barcelona Pavilion and some of Richard Neutra's poetic modern buildings, which blurred the boundary between inside and out. How could Frank Lloyd Wright not be a huge influence: the poetic, earthy quality of his buildings that seemed to grow out of the site; the complete integration of landscape, architecture, interiors, craft, and art; the sense of procession and discovery while moving through his spaces, and the intuitive prospect/refuge dialogue in his spaces that speaks to instinct and creature needs.

Perhaps my all-time favorite building is Louis Kahn's Salk Institute. Its gutsy and powerful use of concrete to frame the ocean has all the power of Luxor Temple. Kahn's sensitive use of light at the Kimbell Art Museum has also had a great influence on my art houses. Then there is Luis Barragán, with his exquisite simplicity and his powerful use of color and light.

In the Pacific Northwest I've been moved by the work of Paul Kirk, which softened "Miesian modernism" with wood, and related to nature like a traditional Japanese pavilion. I admire Roland Terry for his holistic integration of landscape, architecture, interiors, craft, and art, and even lifestyle. In fact, I'm probably more like Roland Terry in approach than anyone else. I've always been moved by the work of Arthur Erickson with his strong lines and use of concrete and wood.

My strongest influence came from my two mentors, architect Ralph Anderson and interior designer Jean Jongeward, with whom I worked while in my twenties. Ralph's skill at crafting exquisite residences and Jean's worldly perspective and insistence on perfection have guided me all my life.

Of course, we are all influenced by our contemporaries, and I note that interior designer Terry Hunziker, with whom I have worked many times, influences my aesthetic. I first met Terry when he

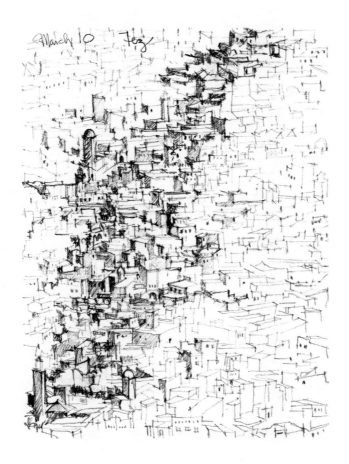

worked for Jean Jongeward early in his career, so we are part of the same "family." The same is true of my longtime friendship with George Suyama, who also worked for Ralph Anderson in the early years.

I recognize that many people in our firm contribute to and influence my designs in a variety of ways—in the drawings, in project team discussions, and at all-office crits. This sharing of ideas and advising one another is an important aspect of who we are as a firm. One person stands out, however, and that is, of course, Tom Kundig. While Tom and I each lead our own projects, we do share the same remarkable firm. I have tremendous admiration for Tom's work and often find myself inspired and emotionally moved by it. His is a kind of subtle, intuitive influence that evolves a little bit every day. Tom's presence, close by, has certainly challenged me and made my work better over all these years.

I have loved to travel throughout my life and am stimulated by experiencing worlds that are very different from my own. I also love my home in America's Pacific Northwest—my sense of this region is a big part of who I am. I try to express the gestalt of my home region when I design here. Its marine climate, the soft light, the beautiful, benevolent natural environment, the historic roots that include Native American traditions and influences from places like Sweden and Japan—all have contributed to a respect for natural materials, a closeness to nature, a certain modesty but a modern, forward-looking attitude. Some call this "warm modernism." When I work in other parts of the world I try to connect to their climate and

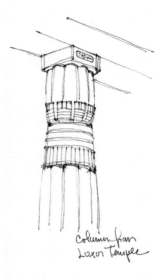

regional cultural influences. In the California desert, we melded with the sagebrush and created large overhangs to shade the house from the sun. In Hong Kong, we created roofs that would shed tropical rains and shade from intense sun. Here, Chinese traditional gardens and architecture were also inspirations. In Atlanta, antebellum architecture was an influence. In London, the historic town and country houses with tall light-catching windows inspired the architecture, while classic English gardens grow right up the facade. The "collection" I've created of grand residences all over the globe interpret certain regional themes and represent a wide range of regions. In every case, I've tried hard to open my architecture to influences of the local climate and culture. One thing I always do is look at historic structures that have stood the test of time, and notice what the materials are, how they were used, and why.

I find that exploring the world through my career as an architect has taken me to places I would never have gone otherwise. I've learned endless amounts from my clients, who in many cases have become lifelong friends. As architects, we are like global ambassadors of goodwill to many friends outside of our country. This experience lifts my holistic view of my profession and the world. We are all connected. We are all part of the same picture, members of the same family.

PAGE 205: Sketch by Olson illustrating the poetic playing off the rational, 2017.
PRECEDING PAGE: Sketch made by Olson during a trip to Fez, Morocco, in 1980.
ABOVE: Olson sketch of Luxor Temple in Egypt, from 1985.

NORTHWEST
ART HOUSE

LOCATION: SEATTLE, WASHINGTON, USA

COMPLETED: 2015

An interest in community and a love of art defines this couple and their Lake Washington home. Passionate art patrons, the clients requested that their extensive collection of glass, sculpture, and two-dimensional art, mostly by Northwest masters, inspire their home's design. I found the owners generous with the design—they conceived of the house for themselves, but also to support the larger art community of which they are a part. The space is designed to be comfortable for two people yet it can also accommodate large groups.

This project is technically a remodeling of an existing house on the property, but the layout and architectural expression are mostly new. We organized the main floor with a long spine from which the living, dining, family, and kitchen areas flow. Art also links the indoors and outdoors, as exterior sculptures and custom glass pieces that delineate the home's entrance draw visitors inside, through the home and to the waterfront terrace and lawn on the other side. Windows throughout offer sweeping views of Lake Washington from the inside, while also framing exterior views of the artwork within. This transparency creates a sense of openness and unity that balances the couple's densely displayed art collection with nature, lake and sky.

The palette of materials is simple—metal panels and stucco on the exterior, with wood and sheet-rock inside. Colors are warm yet neutral to create a subtle backdrop for the art. The clients requested blue tones and materials with sheen and reflectivity, and we also designed furniture to satisfy the clients' unique aesthetic sensibilities. Special, flexible lighting for art is hidden behind ceiling soffits and shelving, and hidden roller shades come down to protect art from sunlight when the owners are away.

The expansiveness of the views and the proximity to Lake Washington make the house feel almost like a houseboat floating on the water. The garden was designed by Allworth Design to make a unified architectural statement with the house. The clients asked us to orient the building so as to preserve a view corridor to Lake Washington for their closest neighbors, and the resulting perpendicular orientation creates an outdoor room. A green roof with sedum and solar panels was specified to meet the clients' environmental concerns.

A dedication to sharing their art with others motivated the couple to incorporate flexible features throughout the home for entertaining, including sliding panels for closing off private areas and emphasizing the central art corridor where guests can linger during gatherings. The main floor of the home primarily consists of spaces for family and guests, while bedrooms and living spaces are located above.

PAGE 209: A long gallery spine connects rooms on the home's main level. **PRECEDING PAGES:** Orienting the house perpendicular to the lake allowed for a large open outdoor space to the south of the home. **OPPOSITE, TOP:** Window walls frame exterior views of the extensive collection of Northwest art. **OPPOSITE, BOTTOM:** The home's neutral exterior palette provides a quiet backdrop for colorful art like this piece by artist Julie Speidel. **ABOVE:** Main level plan.

BAY AREA HILL HOUSE

LOCATION: SAN FRANCISCO BAY AREA, CALIFORNIA, USA

COMPLETED: 2015

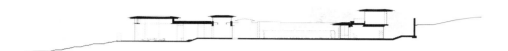

This modern estate crowns a south-facing hill overlooking the Bay Area. The design aims to weave the house into the landscape, and the art and furnishings into the interiors. The result is a continuous, harmonious environment. It takes the form of one large family house broken into smaller houses for cozy, intimate scale, with a grand art gallery spine tying them all together. Rather than being built for a specific collection, the house was designed so an emerging collection could grow into the house. The casual and energetic young family gives life to the formal, refined architecture.

I wanted the house to be grand and elegant but also more delicate than previous houses. Low-key colors provide a background for the art. Long vistas are extended out into the landscape and enlivened by ever-changing pools of water. Family is the connective thread that ties together the three wings of this Bay Area residence. Dividing the home into three areas answered the different "public" and "private" needs of the owners, who have young children but also enjoy entertaining. It has a central pavilion for family gathering and entertaining, and two adjacent wings contain living and sleeping areas for children and guests on one side, and the master suite on the other.

The living room is tall—monumental in scale, yet refined. Wooden ceilings warm the space; soffits block direct sun while bouncing light onto the ceiling to create a warm reflected glow. The use of materials further delineates the spaces, with hardy stone and stucco in the central public areas, contrasted with warm and inviting fir and oak in the more private and intimately scaled adjoining areas. The architecture is modern with highly refined detailing, while the layout is classical, with vistas at every turn.

Balancing the family's art collection with sweeping views of downtown San Francisco that stretch from the Bay Bridge to the Golden Gate Bridge was a key directive for the home's design. Floor-to-ceiling windows, some more than 17 feet (5 m) tall, allow for an encompassing shore-to-sky experience, framing the bay views much like a key piece in the family's art collection. Many artworks are concentrated in the main gallery; however, paintings and sculptures were incorporated into the home's design, with custom panels and niches for art throughout. A few "modern antique" furnishings complement the contemporary art, while we designed custom furniture items and lighting to serve as an extension of the architecture, completing the interior environment.

Outside, a collection of water features including two reflecting pools, designed by landscape architects Surface Design, and a waterfall poetically connect the property to the bay in the distance, with one pool even extending indoors near the home's entrance. Nestled into its hillside location, the home's planted roofs allow it to weave into the hillside, minimizing visual impact. With the high point of the site on the same level as the green roof, this modern estate establishes a deep continuity with the surrounding landscape.

PRECEDING PAGES: South facade. **ABOVE:** Section looking west. **OPPOSITE:** At the home's entrance, an outdoor reflecting pool flows into the interior, visually blurring the distinction between inside and outside.

ABOVE, LEFT: The gallery/colonnade is a "spine" that connects the parts of the house together. On the left is a sculpture by Jeff Koons. **OPPOSITE, RIGHT:** Living room windows frame views of San Francisco. On the coffee table, designed by Jim Olson, is a sculpture by Anish Kapoor.

PRECEDING PAGES: On the dining room wall hangs a piece by the artist Mark Bradford. **OPPOSITE, TOP:** Green roofs and solar panels cap the house as it grows out of the hillside. **OPPOSITE, BOTTOM:** Courtyards and reflecting pools extend the architecture out into the landscape. **ABOVE:** Main level plan. **OVERLEAF:** Concrete columns frame a sculpture by Mark Grotjahn at the west end of the gallery/colonnade.

OPPOSITE, TOP: The sitting room off the master bedroom brings a more intimate scale to the house. The custom coffee table is designed by Jim Olson. OPPOSITE, BOTTOM LEFT: A glass and nickel table sits in the entry. OPPOSITE, BOTTOM RIGHT: The master bathroom opens to views and a private courtyard. ABOVE: A floating soffit in the family room brings a more intimate scale to the lofty space. OVERLEAF: The master bedroom overlooks San Francisco Bay.

TAIWAN VILLAS

LOCATION: TAIPEI, TAIWAN

COMPLETED: 2016

Located in the Great Taipei New Town district in the hills just south of downtown Taipei, the Master Collection is a development of twenty-eight luxury homes. The client's goal was to create a premier neighborhood, using "master" international architects to design the homes, including Richard Meier and Annabelle Selldorf.

From the site you can look down and out across the city lights at night, as well as over seemingly endless tree-covered mountains. That sets the scene—you're living in nature, but you're very close to one of Asia's great cities. Each house was designed to take advantage of its particular site and the views it offered. Some of the sites are flat while others are sloping, but this topography makes the architectural expression more interesting. It's comparable to an Italian hill town—you get these dramatic views that you might not have on a more conventional building site. I was given five houses to design and wanted them to be related, but also for each to be unique. All of the houses are designed to house an art collection, as there is a keen interest in art in Taipei. Each also has a distinct relationship to the lush and serene landscape, and is conceived as a peaceful retreat from the fast pace of the city.

The four-level homes are typically arranged by use: a service level on the lowest level, followed by a casual family level above, a formal entertaining level next, and ending with a private retreat on the top level. The varying topography led to a diversity of architectural expression within the five homes, including several with dramatic vertical interior spaces.

Throughout the homes, large windows frame seamless views, visually dissolving the boundary between inside and outside, an effect further enhanced by infinity-edged pools that merge water and sky. Interior rooms connect to exterior terraces, facilitating cross-ventilation. Deep cantilevered roof planes and generous trellises provide protection from the sun and the elements, yielding elegant interior spaces characterized by soft, dappled light. The expansive, minimal rooms in each home are crafted of stone, stucco, glass, and steel. Strong contrasts between the stone surfaces and more delicate interior features lend a sophisticated character to the homes.

PRECEDING PAGES: The villas crown a hilltop overlooking endless tree-covered mountains. OPPOSITE: The unique architectural expression of each Taiwan Villa is a response to its particular site and views. Stone walls with subtle earth tones tie the buildings to the dramatic site. OVERLEAF: The changing moods of nature as seen from a terrace at Taiwan Villas.

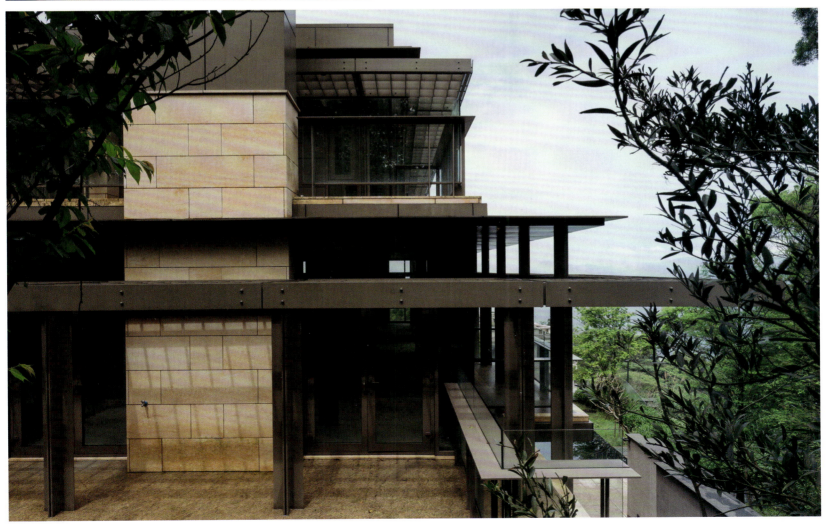

TOFINO
BEACH HOUSE

LOCATION: TOFINO, BRITISH COLUMBIA, CANADA

COMPLETED: 2016

Perched on the westernmost edge of Vancouver Island, Tofino is one of Canada's favorite recreation destinations, where extreme weather conditions draw surfers and storm watchers year round from all over the world. This house was to "grow" out of the magnificent site with its sculptural windblown trees, and provide a focus for beautiful views.

The beach house is filled with light on the south side facing the ocean, and insular and protected on the other side, paneled in dark, rich wood. Glass walls open the living area to panoramic views of forest and ocean, while two fireplaces on either end anchor the space and provide a feeling of cozy refuge. There are no columns or interior structural systems to obscure the view; instead, it feels almost like you are outdoors in a big, open space. The kitchen is in the center of the house—the owner loves cooking and entertaining friends. A small garden courtyard is a microcosm of the rainforest, and the master bedroom looks across a reflecting pool into the woods.

Cantilevering the house six feet (2 m) above grade provides space for ferns and beach salal to grow underneath the glass flooring that runs around the perimeter of the main room, giving the house a sense of floating above the forest floor. The warm, natural tones of the interior take inspiration from Tofino's coastal forest, and are punctuated by pieces from the owner's striking contemporary art collection. Artworks were incorporated into the design of the home, with the fireplace walls specially designed to accommodate paintings by Sam Francis and Diego Singh. I designed a collection of furniture specifically for the house, including a walnut and leather sofa built into the hearth of one fireplace, to complete the interior environment.

Tightknot cedar ceilings in the living area and rich walnut casework in the open kitchen to the rear provide a sense of grounded warmth, which extends to the back bedroom with its dark teak paneling. Here, a vista out over an elevated deck and long reflecting pool offers a second, but different, opportunity for views of water and woods. This house was sited so carefully that only one tree had to be removed during construction, and a green roof above the garage continues the home's natural integration. A nearly continuous line of clerestory windows above the living area required an innovative engineering system for the cantilevered roof, which is held up in only two places by the concrete chimneys. As a result, the roof appears to be floating above the house, which itself is much like a glass boat gliding over a sea of salal.

PRECEDING PAGES: The beach house was sited so carefully that only one tree had to be removed during construction. **OPPOSITE:** The house's entrance is framed by ipe wood screens, which enclose manicured gardens on either side. The screens frame a focused view through the entry to the ocean beyond.

A band of glass flooring surrounds the perimeter of the living area, offering views of salal plants growing below, while reflecting the trees above. The painting above the fireplace is by artist Diego Singh.

BELOW: The kitchen is paneled in rich walnut casework, offering a sense of grounded warmth to the living area. The ceiling "floats" above. **OPPOSITE:** The owner's eclectic art collection, including a painting by Sam Francis, was incorporated into the design.

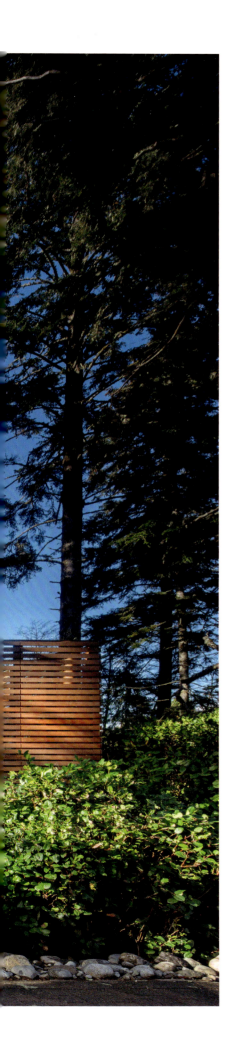

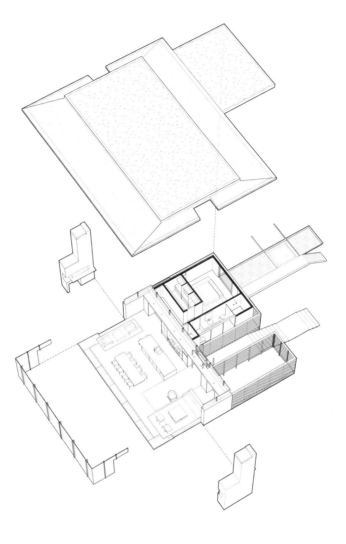

LEFT: The cantilevered roof is structurally supported in only two places by each of the concrete chimneys—it "floats" above the living area. **ABOVE:** Axonometric diagram.
OVERLEAF: A pool extends out from the compact master bedroom, reflecting the sky.
An artwork by Yayoi Kusama hangs above the bed.

HUDSON VALLEY
RESIDENCE

LOCATION: WESTCHESTER, NEW YORK, USA

COMPLETED: 2017

Perched high on a hill, this country house overlooks the clients' property—14 acres (8 hectares) in New York State—as well as forested hills, distant country houses, reservoirs, and fields of grazing horses. The clients had seen my Hong Kong Villa in *Architectural Digest*, which was a grand house that also deferred to nature. For this project we started on one site, then the clients decided they preferred another. The new site was already home to a historic mansion, and after a couple of years of trying to incorporate it, we decided to use its belfry as a guesthouse, which makes a perfect home for visiting children and grandchildren.

The clients were personally and passionately involved throughout the design process, making this house a particularly collaborative effort. All together we designed at least four houses, studying views, sun angles, sound abatement, and so on, to end up with a final design. Framed around views of the site, the design of this weekend home is based on classic proportions while incorporating elements appropriate to its rural East Coast setting. Stone chimneys and fireplaces are juxtaposed with modern materials such as steel and copper, while a formal entry sequence through a courtyard opens to a suspended, triple-height steel staircase. This integration of tradition and modernity lends a stately balance to the home, which is presented as an elegant object surrounded by expansive lawns.

Because you drive onto the site and soon see the house up at the top of the hill, the exterior composition of the home is important. Meanwhile, on the interior, as in many of my houses, formal circulation patterns create framed vistas of the garden and countryside. The residence is organized into two levels and a basement, with several outdoor terraces extending off the ground-level rooms. Upon entering the home, a long promenade corridor extends in either direction, housing works from the owners' collections of art and Asian porcelain. Every vista ends in a framed view of nature, subtly recalling the floral themes that decorate the porcelain pieces, and all views are complemented by the classic proportions of the home. A formal living room on the main level is almost a standalone pavilion, with sliding window walls on both sides, and a double-soffit ceiling with clerestory windows that accentuate the lofty verticality of the space. An informal family room on the western prow of the home is capped by the master suite above, yielding breathtaking views from both rooms all the way down to the nearby reservoir. Auxiliary spaces include two guest rooms on the main level and three on the floor above, along with an upper-level exercise room, art studio, and office and, like all the rooms in the house, they each enjoy a special view of nature.

PRECEDING PAGES: West facade. OPPOSITE: The home's main promenade terminates at each end in a framed vista of the landscape.

OPPOSITE: The living room is a more formal space with layered soffits and a tall, "infinite" ceiling. **ABOVE:** Main level plan.

ABOVE, LEFT: In the office on the home's upper level, full-height window walls give the feeling of floating in the tree canopy. **OPPOSITE, RIGHT:** The informal family room extending from the home's western prow opens to a panoramic view. Furniture is by Ben Erickson. **OVERLEAF:** View of family room and master bedroom wing from the entry drive.

FUNCTIONS OF SPACE

I set out to solve functional problems in my designs, and I want my architecture to be the best that it can be in every way. It is my belief that houses and other buildings should shelter us from the elements, materials should last for generations, and the flow of space should accommodate the many rituals of everyday life.

Going into greater detail, the temperature inside should be pleasant, lighting should fit the desired mood and be flexible enough to adapt when that mood changes, and furniture should be comfortable. Stairs should have deep treads and shallow risers when possible to make climbing them an elegant, effortless experience. Kitchens should be arranged for efficiency. Bathroom floors should be warm, there should be a ledge for a coffee cup and a newspaper, and shower floors should be rough enough to prevent slipping. Bedrooms should be quiet with good ventilation. Views must be maximized from the living rooms, but paintings should be protected from ultraviolet rays. Roofs shouldn't leak, and there should be protection above windows to prevent stains from rainwater. The list of details to consider seems endless, but each tiny thing means a great deal when it comes to everyday graceful living.

When I design a house (or a public building, for that matter) I picture myself in the space. I draw and erase, draw and erase, draw and erase as my intuitive side slowly guides my rational side. I follow my feelings about how something looks and feels until it is just right. I always draw furniture in floor plans, even early on, and often include small human figures to scale—always imagining that I am in the space, feeling it as though it were already real. I work hard to protect the functionality of spaces while the artist in me endeavors to make them beautiful: the scale, the colors and textures, the views, and the sunlight are the "paints" I have on my palette.

Architecture is about living, and living usually involves movement. While designing, I always consider the experience of the space. I don't think of my architecture as a "building" or "object," but rather as a vehicle for experiencing life—whether moving through the interior or noticing the external environment. I have great admiration for the tradition of Japanese gardens, where the environment unfolds as you stroll sequentially through the space. Each encounter sets you up for the next, and the whole experience opens up your awareness to the world around you as it stimulates the senses. I also love to move through ritualistic formal spaces like ancient Egyptian temples or Gothic cathedrals. My houses often combine the formal movement of the Egyptian temple with the more poetic movement of the Japanese garden. A balance

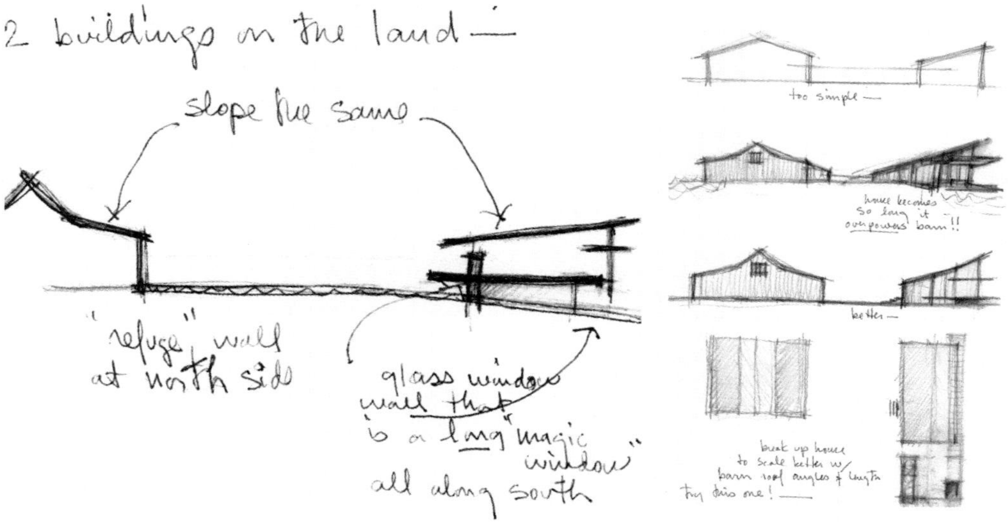
2 buildings on the land —
slope the same
"refuge" wall
at north side
glass window wall that
is a long "magic window"
all along south
too simple —
house becomes
so long it
overpowers barn!!
better —
break up house
to scale better w/
barn roof angles & length
try this one! —

PRECEDING PAGE: Olson sketch overlaid on computer rendering of Bay Area Hill House, San Francisco Bay Area, California, sketch done in 2011. **ABOVE:** Explorations in shape sketched by Olson for Glass Farmhouse, eastern Oregon, sketch done in 2006.

between the two is evident in many of my projects. Following are some of the typical experiences I try to create.

What we see when we approach the building sets us up for the whole experience. Walking toward the door might feel like a procession, and as the front door is revealed, it is like discovering a precious jewel. The handle is carefully crafted, long and elegant, fitting comfortably in our hand. On opening the door we see through the building to a view beyond, perhaps looking onto a courtyard, or we might focus on a powerful piece of art. Passing through the doorway over the threshold is a key experience.

Often a circulation "spine" that connects the various rooms of a house (or building) can take on great importance. I like to accentuate the length of a space by creating vistas that draw our eyes outside across the landscape—sometimes, reflecting pools further dramatize this experience. Walking down such a corridor can feel ceremonial. Columns along the way can set up a cadence as we move, helping us to feel the space as we pass through it.

While the hallway is about movement, the rooms themselves are usually about being still—to be experienced like nests. In living rooms I think about creature comforts. These are refuges from which we can see out over the landscape and be stimulated, and yet we are safe and private, enclosed from behind. Human scale is important here, as well as soft, comfortable materials.

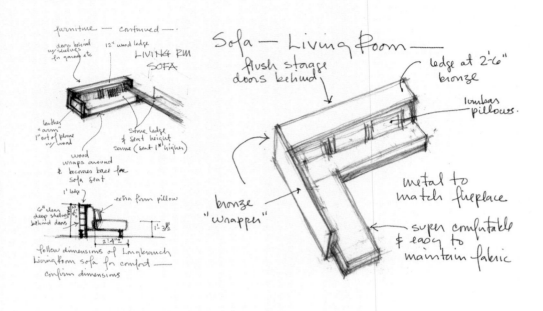

The living room should bring people together, providing a sense of "hearth." It is a warm, central place that looks inward as well as outward, with comfortable seating designed to encourage conversation and arranged to be inclusive. Soft, pleasant lighting helps us to feel comfortable and at ease.

Early in my projects I become emotionally attached to my imagined walks through these future spaces. I get a kind of warm glow inside when it is right, sensing it by instinct. Is this how a bird feels when its nest is just right? Two or three years later, when the project is finished and I walk through the space or look at it from the outside, I get that same internal glow. It's a feeling similar to love—not an egotistical feeling, but one of extreme warmth for the "creation." It's this feeling that keeps me on the path of architecture, year after year after year.

ABOVE: Sofa designs by Olson for California Meadow House, Woodside, California, 2013, and for Tofino Beach House, Tofino, British Columbia, sketch done in 2014.

CALIFORNIA MEADOW HOUSE

LOCATION: SAN FRANCISCO BAY AREA, CALIFORNIA, USA

COMPLETED: 2017

Envisioned as a single continuous, flowing expression, this family estate links architecture, interior design, art, and landscape into an integrated whole. The client wanted the entry sequence to be a "slow reveal," so the driveway winds through a grove of olive trees and the house is seen sequentially.

The site is flat and spacious with views into the nearby mountains. This house is about outdoor living—whether actually being outdoors, or opening up the indoors to the outside. The space is intended for a friendly, fun-loving family with three children, as well as their extended family and lots of friends—they love to entertain. The program features a variety of spaces for entertaining and hosting philanthropic and political events, including a dining room for up to fifty people, and an outdoor dining table in the vineyard.

Around the central living area, views radiate in four directions across several reflecting pools to vistas into gardens and the nearby Santa Cruz Mountains. The residence also includes three auxiliary buildings and extensive outdoor living areas, but the subdued quality of the design helps blend the home into its verdant site. The spaces created between the home's various structures engage with the landscape.

The 3.5-acre (1-hectare) site is organized into two interconnected parts, reflecting contrasting attitudes toward the landscape. Along the entry to the property, rows of old-growth olive trees, a small vineyard and a succulent garden suggest a human touch. This cultivated portion of the site contains the "public" areas of the house, including the main living and dining area. Continuing this "public" space are the three auxiliary buildings, which step back along the front of the property perpendicular to the main house, echoing the organized rows of the nearby vineyard. These buildings include a two-bedroom guesthouse, an outdoor living pavilion, and a dining pavilion with an underground pub.

The other side of the site, delineated by an infinity pool and gentle slope, opens into uncultivated meadow space. This more "wild" half of the site contains the private areas of the home, designed for quiet relaxation and dreaming, including the master suite, office, and three children's bedrooms.

On both sides of the site, a fluidity between inside and outside defines the built environment. Retracting window walls—including a U-shaped window around the dining pavilion that lowers completely into the ground—open much of the home to nature, maximizing outdoor living possibilities and natural ventilation. Trellises weave over these spaces, providing shade from the California sun and further blending the home into the landscape.

An earthy exterior palette of patinated bronze, black granite, and dark wood inspired by the California woodland setting continues inside the home. I designed a collection of custom furniture especially for this house. Lighting integrates with the interior environment. We also helped curate an international contemporary art collection for the home, complementing its architectural expression. Designed to produce as much energy as it uses ("net zero"), the house incorporates several high-performance systems, including solar panels covering over half of the roof area, and geothermal and hydronic heating and cooling systems. The result is a home integrated with nature, not only philosophically and visually, but from a practical perspective as well.

PAGE 261: View of the house from the swimming pool. PRECEDING PAGES: The house is entered past cascading reflecting pools. OPPOSITE: In the living room, a collection of custom furniture designed by Jim Olson helps link architecture, interior design, and art in an integrated whole. The fireplace and chimney are bronze. OVERLEAF: Hallway looking toward the main entrance from the lounge, with the living room on the left.

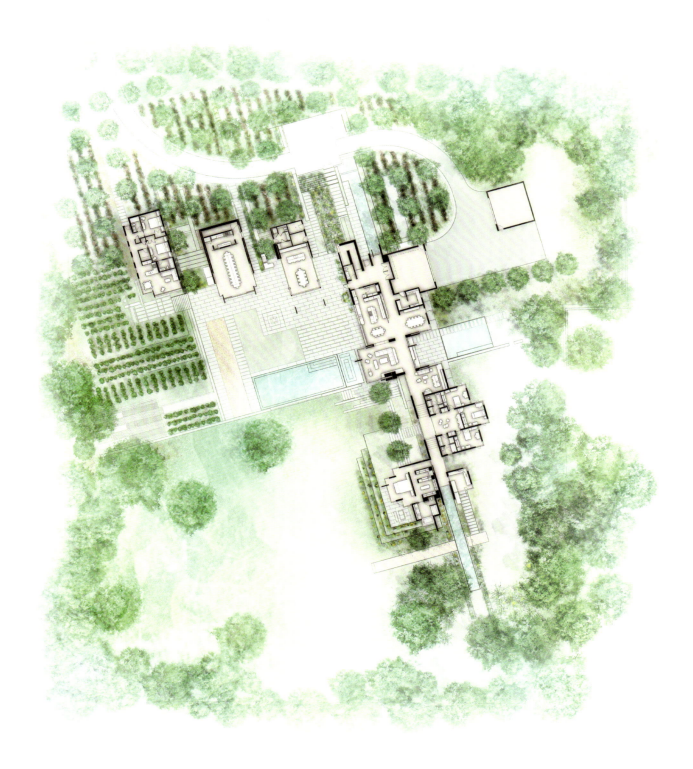

OPPOSITE: The home's main dining and living area opens to an outdoor terrace with gardens and a swimming pool, with a small vineyard just beyond. **ABOVE:** Main floor plan and site plan.

KIRKLAND MUSEUM OF FINE & DECORATIVE ART

LOCATION: DENVER, COLORADO, USA

COMPLETED: IN PROGRESS

PRECEDING PAGES: The newest
addition to Denver's Golden Triangle,
the Kirkland joins the Denver Art
Museum, the Clyfford Still Museum,
and others. OPPOSITE, TOP:
Strong horizontal floating planes
play off the vertical texture of the
terracotta facade. OPPOSITE,
BOTTOM: A series of vitrines
mounted onto the exterior of the
building showcase selected objects
from the museum's collection, and
a bronze sculpture by Edgar Britton
further extends the museum's
galleries to neighboring sidewalks.
ABOVE: Main level plan.

Kirkland Museum of Fine & Decorative Art is in the heart of Denver's museum district, known as the Golden Triangle. It is located across the street from the Denver Art Museum and the Clyfford Still Museum, but despite this grand location it stays true to the intimate atmosphere for which Kirkland has always been known, offering visitors an enhanced salon-like experience. Merle Chambers Fund provided the funding for the new two-storey building that highlights the artistry and craft of the museum's internationally renowned decorative art collection, and its singular collection of art by Colorado artists.

The museum is named for renowned Colorado artist Vance Kirkland, whose historic studio building is part of the museum. The museum director had known Kirkland, and upon Kirkland's death was willed the contents of Kirkland's studio, which included many Kirkland paintings, and his collection of decorative arts and artworks by many of Colorado's best artists. Over the years, the museum expanded the decorative and fine art collections, which now comprise over 30,000 works, including the nation's largest repository of Colorado art, and the International Decorative Art Collection, which is considered one of the most important design collections in North America.

I wanted the building to represent the richness of the art and crafts that it would house, and I hoped that the architecture itself would be an important piece in the decorative arts collection. Because so many of the pieces in the collection were intended for domestic use, the scale of the building reflects this—I want people to feel as if they are touring a grand home. The museum likes to display art salon-style and very dense, quite different than typical contemporary museums—and the result is a cozy, disarming environment that inspires affection in visitors. The aim is for people to feel that they have just visited a charming modern home filled with treasures of art and design. The new museum has a total of thirteen galleries. While the elevations are calm and the layout is straightforward and easy to navigate, the materials cladding the exterior are full of energy. A key element of the design is a rich and vibrant facade inspired by the lively mix of art and craft in the collection. Luminous terracotta bars in an array of yellow hues, punctuated by rectangular glass "baguettes" backed in gold, enliven the building's public face, sparkling in the bright Colorado sunlight, and recalling the energy of a Vance Kirkland painting. A series of vitrines mounted onto the exterior of the building also showcase selected objects from the museum's collection, extending the galleries to the neighboring sidewalks and streets.

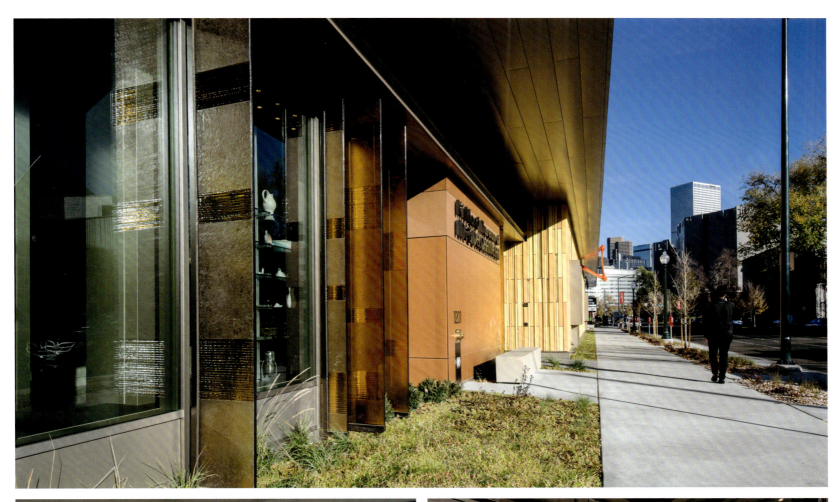

OPPOSITE, TOP: Robert Mangold's 1982 sculpture, "Double Tetrahedralhypershere No. 41" is installed on the Kirkland's façade. **OPPOSITE, BOTTOM:** At night, the museum lobby glows from within, illuminating the glass and ceramic objects on display in the windows. **TOP:** Windows showcase objects from the collection and extend the galleries onto the neighboring sidewalk. **BOTTOM, LEFT:** A vignette from the previous Kirkland Museum that will be replicated in the new building. **BOTTOM, RIGHT:** Inside the museum's lobby, reflections on the terrazzo floors merge sky, façade, and art objects.

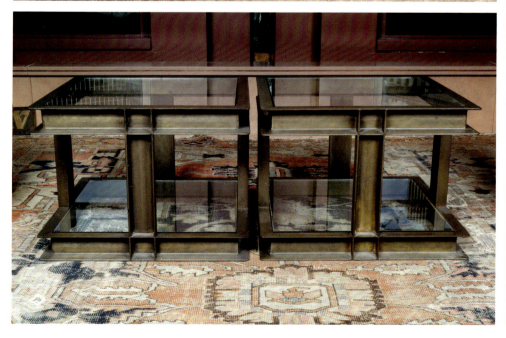

CUSTOM FURNITURE

 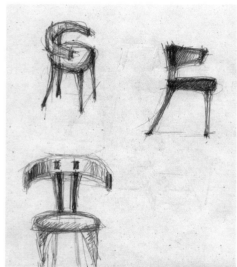

I see furniture as part of the holistic environment—landscape, architecture, interiors, furniture, and art; a piece of a larger whole. I also see it as an extension of the architecture at times, and a counterpoint to the architecture at other times. For me, furniture must be comfortable and functional, as well as beautiful, to be successful. In some ways, furniture can live longer than typical architecture, because it is portable and adaptable to new environments. Good flexible furniture is like good art; it becomes more valuable with age. I started designing furniture in my thirties. It was always site-specific, but many of the early pieces have since been adapted to new environments. I've always found it hard to find well-designed furnishings for my houses, so this need led me to design many custom pieces. Until now, each piece has been one of a kind for a specific location, but I'm now in the process of designing a line of furniture—a new experience. I'm trying to make it changeable and adaptable so it can become personal and appropriate for each individual owner.

PAGE 276: Custom tables, designed by Jim Olson for (clockwise from top left) Northwoods House, Olson Condominium, Decorative Arts House, Glass Apartment, Olson Condominium, and Longbranch Cabin. PAGE 277: Capital House (top), Exhibition table (bottom). ABOVE: Jim Olson sketches of a bronze chair for Decorative Arts House (left) and a bronze and wood chair for Glass Apartment (right). OPPOSITE: A series of custom chairs designed by Jim Olson for (clockwise from top left) Decorative Arts House, Hong Kong Villa, Glass Apartment, and Longbranch Cabin.

EXHIBITS

There have been three exhibits of my work: one at Washington State University Museum of Art (2011), one at the Lightcatcher (2013), and one at the University of Washington's College of Built Environments (2016). We designed the exhibits; I collaborated with William Franklin on those at Washington State University and the Lightcatcher (which he led), while Laura Bartunek led the one at the University of Washington. The Washington State University and Lightcatcher exhibits were generated by Chris Bruce, then the director of the Museum of Art at Washington State University. They were intended to explore the way I had created architecture for art, and in both cases we tried to create a sense of scale, order, and elegance that demonstrated the character of the various houses I'd designed for art and art collections. We used photographs (large, life-like scale), small models, drawings, and actual art pieces from my clients' collections, and did everything we could to help people feel as if they were actually in the spaces. I especially valued the chance to share the private worlds I'd created with the public—and also to share the richness and variety of the amazing art collections, and my own love of art, with others.

The exhibit at the University of Washington used my own retreat at Longbranch as the centerpiece. Because I started the cabin when I was a student (eighteen years old) at the University of Washington School of Architecture, the students could relate my career to their own lives. The exhibit showed the cabin at its four stages of construction and showed other projects I was working on at each stage. The cabin/retreat at Longbranch really represents my life and my career—from teenager to old man. I like to think, too, that my love of ART and NATURE come out in these exhibits.

PRECEDING PAGES: The Washington State University Museum of Art exhibit included a mural of Longbranch Cabin (left) and several art pieces from Olson's clients (right), whose art collections are displayed in Olson's houses. **OPPOSITE, TOP AND BOTTOM LEFT:** "Jim Olson: Home Base" exhibit at the University of Washington's College of Built Environments. **OPPOSITE, BOTTOM RIGHT:** "Jim Olson: Art in Architecture" exhibit at the Lightcatcher at the Whatcom Museum. **OVERLEAF:** The "Jim Olson: Art in Architecture" exhibit at the Museum of Art at Washington State University contained a small pavilion, designed by Olson, with a mural by artist Mary Ann Peters for a complete art immersion experience.

COMPLETE CHRONOLOGY
OF WORKS

1950s

LONGBRANCH CABIN
Longbranch, Washington
Completed: 1959

1960s

THOMPSON TRELLIS
Key Center, Washington
Completed: c. 1963-1964

RIPLEY BUNKHOUSE
Lakebay, Washington
Completed: 1964

LEVINE ART STUDIO
Burien, Washington
Completed: c. 1965

HANSON RESIDENCE REMODEL
Seattle, Washington
Completed: c. 1965

OLSON RESIDENCE
Toppenish, Washington
Completed: c. 1965

CONRY RESIDENCE
Longbranch, Washington
Completed: 1966

YOUNG RESIDENCE
Mercer Island, Washington
Completed: 1966

FOREMAN RESIDENCE REMODEL
Beaux Arts Village, Washington
Completed: 1966

MT. BAKER TOWNHOUSE
(With Gordon Walker)
Seattle, Washington
Completed: 1966

WHITE RESIDENCE REMODEL
Tacoma, Washington
Completed: 1968

PENFIELD RESIDENCE
Longbranch, Washington
Completed: 1968

ARMSTRONG RESIDENCE
Chehalis, Washington
Completed: 1968

BAIRD RESIDENCE
Seattle, Washington
Completed: late 1960s

CAMPBELL RESIDENCE REMODEL
Seattle, Washington
Completed: 1968

SHUPP DUPLEX
Sitka, Alaska
Completed: late 1960s

**OLSON WALKER,
MAUD BUILDING OFFICE (1969–1974)**
(With Gordon Walker)
Seattle, Washington
Completed: 1969

THONN RESIDENCE
Seattle, Washington
Completed: 1969

THONN TABLE DESIGN
Seattle, Washington
Completed: 1969

1970s

MOWAT RESIDENCE
Clyde Hill, Washington
Completed: 1970

LYCETTE RESIDENCE REMODEL
Clyde Hill, Washington
Completed: 1970

KENMORE PARK
(With Gordon Walker)
Kenmore, Washington
Completed: c. 1971

LAKE CITY PLAYGROUND PARK
(With Gordon Walker)
Seattle, Washington
Completed: c. 1971

OLSON RESIDENCE
Seattle, Washington
Completed: 1972

RICHARDS RESIDENCE
Gig Harbor, Washington
Completed: 1972

FREEMAN RESIDENCE REMODEL
Seattle, Washington
Completed: 1972

IRWIN RESIDENCE
Renton, Washington
Completed: 1974

OLSON WALKER,
NATIONAL BUILDING OFFICE (1974–1980)
(With Gordon Walker)
Seattle, Washington
Completed: 1974

PAGE RESIDENCE REMODEL
Burien, Washington
Completed: 1974

POLSON RESIDENCE
Tacoma, Washington
Completed: 1974

CAMPBELL RESIDENCE
Seattle, Washington
Completed: 1974

SHELTER HOUSE, SEATTLE PARKS
Seattle, Washington
Completed: 1974

PESSEMIER RESIDENCE
Tacoma, Washington
Completed: 1974

BOVINGTON RESIDENCE REMODEL
Seattle, Washington
Completed: c. 1975

AL AND LEON'S FURNITURE
Seattle, Washington
Completed: c. 1975

BOESKOV RESIDENCE
Clyde Hill, Washington
Completed: 1975

SALAD GALLERY RESTAURANT
Seattle, Washington
Completed: 1975

REMODEL OF SUNSET CLUB
(Assisted Jean Jongeward)
Seattle, Washington
Completed: c. 1975

LYON RESIDENCE
Tacoma, Washington
Completed: 1975

WOLFF RESIDENCE
Hillsborough, California
Completed: 1975

BUCKNER NEWS ALLIANCE OFFICE
Seattle, Washington
Completed: 1976

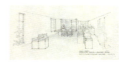

MCKENZIE RIGNEY JEWELRY STORE
Tacoma, Washington
Completed: 1976

ATLANTIC STREET VETERINARY HOSPITAL
Seattle, Washington
Completed: 1976

FRYBERGER FLOATING HOME
Seattle, Washington
Completed: 1976

MOWAT RESIDENCE
Hunts Point, Washington
Completed: 1976

TALLAHAN RESIDENCE
Seattle, Washington
Completed: 1977

CARLSON RESIDENCE
Borrego Springs, California
Completed: 1977

WILLIAMS RESIDENCE REMODEL
Seattle, Washington
Completed: 1977

BAGLEY WRIGHT OFFICE
(Assisted Jean Jongeward)
Seattle, Washington
Completed: c. 1978

FORDYCE RESIDENCE REMODEL
Seattle, Washington
Completed: 1978

PIKE & VIRGINIA BUILDING
(Jim Olson, lead designer, with Gordon Walker
and Rick Sundberg)
Seattle, Washington
Completed: 1978

**OLSON CONDOMINIUM,
PIKE & VIRGINIA BUILDING**
Seattle, Washington
Completed: 1978

**FURNITURE, OLSON CONDOMINIUM,
PIKE & VIRGINIA BUILDING**
Seattle, Washington
Completed: 1978

**PETERSON RESIDENCE,
PIKE & VIRGINIA BUILDING**
Seattle, Washington
Completed: 1978

**R. DAVID ADAMS FLOWERS,
PIKE & VIRGINIA BUILDING**
Seattle, Washington
Completed: 1978

**LAWENDA CONDOMINIUM,
PIKE & VIRGINIA BUILDING**
Seattle, Washington
Completed: 1978

**BROWN CONDOMINIUM,
PIKE & VIRGINIA BUILDING**
Seattle, Washington
Completed: 1978

FREEMAN RESIDENCE REMODEL
Bellevue, Washington
Completed: 1978

HANSON RESIDENCE REMODEL
Seattle, Washington
Completed: 1979

O'BYRNE RESIDENCE REMODEL
Hunts Point, Washington
Completed: 1979

CARKONEN APARTMENTS
Seattle, Washington
Completed: 1979

1980s

OLSON WALKER, HILLCLIMB OFFICE (1980–1987)
(With Gordon Walker)
Seattle, Washington
Completed: 1980

SUNDAY COVE CONDOMINIUM
(With Gordon Walker)
Bainbridge Island, Washington
Completed: 1980

BARN RESIDENCE
Lakebay, Washington
Completed: c. 1980

STEWART BUILDING
(With Rick Sundberg)
Seattle, Washington
Completed: 1980

SCHMIDT RESIDENCE
Seattle, Washington
Completed: 1981

OLSON CONDOMINIUM
Tacoma, Washington
Completed: 1980

REED MCCLURE OFFICE
Seattle, Washington
Completed: c. 1980

FAAS RESIDENCE REMODEL
Mercer Island, Washington
Completed: 1980

LONGBRANCH CABIN ADDITION
Longbranch, Washington
Completed: 1981

WILEY RESIDENCE
Orcas Island, Washington
Completed: 1981

RESIDENCE REMODELS
Medina, Washington
Phases completed: 1981, 1982, 1989, 1997, 1999

CONCEPTS FOR SEATTLE
(Hewitt/Daly, Olson/Walker, Hobbs/Fukui/Davison, Barnett
Schorr/Miller, Dan Calvin: *The Weekly*)
Seattle, Washington
Completed: 1981—82

FLOATING HOME
Portland, Oregon
Completed: 1982

**51 UNIVERSITY STREET
BUILDING REMODEL**
Seattle, Washington
Completed: 1981

THE PEAK COMPETITION
Hong Kong, China
Completed: 1982

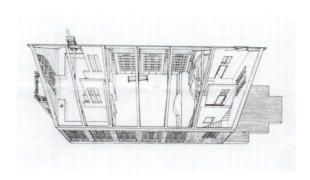

CHURCH RESIDENCE REMODEL
Seattle, Washington
Completed: c. 1984

STEWART BROTHERS COFFEE
Seattle, Washington
Completed: 1982

LEVY RESIDENCE
Mercer Island, Washington
Completed: 1982

JAMES TURRELL EXHIBITION AT COCA
(Assisted James Turrell)
Center on Contemporary Art, Seattle, Washington
Completed: 1982

COMMUTER BUILDING PROJECT
Seattle, Washington
Completed: 1984; unbuilt

MUSEUM IN THE CITY DESIGN COMPETITION
(With Jeffrey Bishop, Nancy Mee, Dennis Evans, and Keith Beckley)
Seattle, Washington
Completed: 1984; unbuilt

HARRISON RIDGE PROJECT, 32ND & EAST DENNY
(Olson/Walker, Hewitt/Daly, Hobbs/Fukui, Streeter, Calvin/Gorasht)
Seattle, Washington
Completed: 1985; unbuilt

**NC MACHINERY
CORPORATE HEADQUARTERS**
Tukwila, Washington
Completed: 1985

**LAW OFFICES OF REED, MCCLURE,
MOCERI, THONN, AND MORIARTY**
Seattle, Washington
Completed: 1985

**SOUTH ARCADE,
98 UNION BUILDING**
(With Rick Sundberg)
Seattle, Washington
Completed: 1985

**RESIDENCE,
98 UNION BUILDING**
Seattle, Washington
Completed: 1985

WRAY RESIDENCE
Federal Way, Washington
Completed: 1986

BLAKELY ISLAND RETREAT
Blakely Island, Washington
Completed: 1986

OAK TREE CINEMA
Seattle, Washington
Completed: 1986

NORTHSTREAM BUILDING
Kirkland, Washington
Completed: 1986

OLYMPIC BLOCK
(Olson/Walker, Hewitt/Daly)
Seattle, Washington
Completed: 1986

ALBERT PROJECT
Seattle, Washington
Completed: 1986; unbuilt

RESIDENCE REMODEL
Portland, Oregon
Completed: 1987

RESIDENCE REMODEL
Seattle, Washington
Completed: 1987

 LEWIS RESIDENCE
(With Tom Kundig)
Federal Way, Washington
Completed: 1987

MONROE JEWELER
(With Tom Kundig)
Seattle, Washington
Completed: 1987

GALLERY HOUSE
Seattle, Washington
Completed: 1987

 ST. BARNABAS EPISCOPAL CHURCH PROJECT
Bainbridge Island, Washington
Completed: 1987; unbuilt

**UNIVERSITY STREET LOCAL IMPROVEMENT
DISTRICT PROJECT**
Seattle, Washington
Completed: 1987; unbuilt

 TABLE
Seattle, Washington
Completed: 1987

**OLSON SUNDBERG,
CITY CLUB BUILDING OFFICE (1987–2001)**
(With Rick Sundberg)
Seattle, Washington
Completed: 1987

OLSON CONDOMINIUM
Seattle, Washington
Completed: 1987

DESK
Seattle, Washington
Completed: 1988

RESIDENCE
(With Tom Kundig)
Seattle, Washington
Completed: 1988

ANDERSON RESIDENCE
Seattle, Washington
Phases completed: 1988, 1996, 2001

RESIDENCE
Hunts Point, Washington
Completed: 1988

BABB REMODEL
Bend, Oregon
Completed: 1988

RESIDENCE REMODEL
Seattle, Washington
Completed: 1988

STEWART BROTHERS COFFEE
Seattle, Washington
Completed: 1988

OVERLAKE PARK PRESBYTERIAN CHURCH
Bellevue, Washington
Completed: 1989

**WASHINGTON STATE
CAPITOL MUSEUM STUDY**
Olympia, Washington
Completed: 1989; unbuilt

1990s

UNITY CHURCH PROJECT
Bellevue, Washington
Completed: 1990; unbuilt

BEACH HOUSE REMODEL
(With Tom Kundig)
Seattle, Washington
Completed: 1990

MODERN VILLA
Lake Forest, Illinois
Completed: 1990

RESIDENCE REMODEL
Hunts Point, Washington
Completed: 1991

SEATTLE'S BEST COFFEE
Seattle, Washington
Completed: 1991

ONE CARILLON POINT
Kirkland, Washington
Completed: 1991

**BERNARD CONDOMINIUM,
CARILLON POINT**
Kirkland, Washington
Completed: 1991

**HEALTHY CONDOMINIUM,
CARILLON POINT**
Kirkland, Washington
Completed: 1991

RESIDENCE REMODEL
Seattle, Washington
Completed: 1991

**MEMORY ROOM,
RESIDENCE ADDITION**
Seattle, Washington
Completed: 1991

SEATTLE ART MUSEUM
(Assisted Robert Venturi as local architect)
Seattle, Washington
Completed: 1991

**THONN RESIDENCE
REMODEL AND ADDITION**
Seattle, Washington
Completed: 1991

HAUBERG RESIDENCE
(With Tom Kundig)
Seattle, Washington
Completed: 1991

**RUG AND FURNITURE DESIGN, HAUBERG
RESIDENCE**
Seattle, Washington
Completed: 1991

     DOG THRONE
Seattle, Washington
Completed: 1992

**BEHNKE CONDOMINIUM,
CARILLON POINT**
Kirkland, Washington
Completed: 1992

URBAN NATURE HOUSE REMODEL
Seattle, Washington
Completed: 1992

DONNELLY RESIDENCE
Seattle, Washington
Completed: 1992

BLUFF HOUSE
(With Tom Kundig)
Seattle, Washington
Completed: 1992

NOAH ART STUDIO
(With Alan Maskin)
Seattle, Washington
Completed: 1992

RESIDENCE REMODEL
Bainbridge Island, Washington
Completed: 1992

SAMMAMISH HILLS LUTHERAN CHURCH CONCEPT STUDIES PROJECT
Sammamish, Washington
Completed: c. 1992; unbuilt

WOOD CONDOMINIUM, CARILLON POINT
Kirkland, Washington
Completed: 1993

PRAIRIE HOUSE
Highland Park, Illinois
Completed: 1993

RESIDENCE REMODEL
Seattle, Washington
Completed: 1993

RESIDENCE REMODEL
Longbranch, Washington
Completed: 1993

WOODLAND PARK ZOO ENTRANCE
Seattle, Washington
Completed: 1993

DIFFA (DESIGN INDUSTRIES FOUNDATION FIGHTING AIDS) JACKET
Seattle, Washington
Completed: 1994

FIRST HILL EXHIBIT
(With Alan Maskin)
Seattle, Washington
Completed: 1994

GURUDWARA SINGH SABHA SIKH TEMPLE CONCEPT STUDIES PROJECT
Renton, Washington
Completed: 1994; unbuilt

COTTAGE REMODEL
Lopez Island, Washington
Completed: 1994

WRIGHT CONDOMINIUM, CARILLON POINT
Kirkland, Washington
Completed: 1995

EXPERIENCE MUSIC PROJECT CONCEPT STUDIES
Seattle, Washington
Completed: 1995

SHELTER HOUSE
(With Tom Kundig)
Mercer Island, Washington
Completed: 1995

YAKIMA VALLEY HOUSE
Yakima, Washington
Completed: 1995

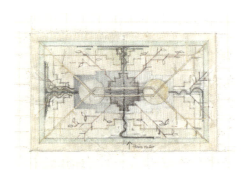

**RUG AND FURNITURE DESIGN,
YAKIMA VALLEY HOUSE**
Yakima, Washington
Completed: 1995

**CONDOMINIUM,
CARILLON POINT**
Kirkland, Washington
Completed: 1995

BELLEVUE ART MUSEUM EXHIBITION
(Assisted with Jean Jongeward exhibit)
Bellevue, Washington
Completed: 1995

RESIDENCE CONCEPTS
Vashon Island, Washington
Completed: 1995; unbuilt

**CABIN,
BLISS LANDING**
British Columbia, Canada
Completed: 1995

TEMPLE B'NAI TORAH
Bellevue, Washington
Completed: 1995; unbuilt

HANSON CONDOMINIUM
Seattle, Washington
Completed: 1996

THE CLIFF REMODEL
Longbranch, Washington
Completed: 1996

RESIDENCE REMODEL
Orcas Island, Washington
Completed: 1996

RESIDENCE
San Juan Island, Washington
Completed: 1997

WEST WALL REMODEL,
ST. MARK'S EPISCOPAL CATHEDRAL
Seattle, Washington
Completed: 1997

GARDEN HOUSE
Atherton, California
Completed: 1998

THOMPSON CHAPEL ALTAR,
ST. MARK'S EPISCOPAL CATHEDRAL
Seattle, Washington
Completed: 1997

RED HOUSE
Denver, Colorado
Completed: 1998

MEDINA RESIDENCE REMODEL
Medina, Washington
Completed: c. 1997

RESIDENCE PROJECT
Kirkland, Washington
Completed: 1998; unbuilt

LONGBRANCH CABIN ADDITION
Longbranch, Washington
Completed: 1997

PORTAGE BAY HOUSE
Seattle, Washington
Completed: 1999

RESIDENCE PROJECT
Austin, Texas
Completed: 1999; unbuilt

ZEN HOUSE
Seattle, Washington
Completed: 1999

NORTHMINSTER PRESBYTERIAN CHURCH
Seattle, Washington
Completed: 1999

DESERT HOUSE
Palm Desert, California
Completed: 1999

WRIGHT EXHIBITION SPACE
(With Richard Gluckman Consulting)
Seattle, Washington
Completed: 1999

2000s

MARKET APARTMENT
Seattle, Washington
Completed: 2000

OLSON RESIDENCE ADDITION
Seattle, Washington
Completed: 2000

SEATTLE ASIAN ART MUSEUM
Seattle, Washington
Completed: 2000

RESIDENCE REMODEL
Seattle, Washington
Completed: 2000

RESIDENCE
Samish Island, Washington
Completed: 2000

CONDOMINIUM
Seattle, Washington
Completed: 2000

RESIDENCE PROJECT
Mercer Island, Washington
Completed: 2001

GIG HARBOR HERITAGE CENTER PROJECT
Gig Harbor, Washington
Completed: 2001; unbuilt

RESIDENCE REMODEL
Seattle, Washington
Completed: 2001

SALT LAKE CITY HOUSE
Salt Lake City, Utah
Completed: 2001

GLASS APARTMENT
Seattle, Washington
Completed: 2001

FURNITURE DESIGN, GLASS APARTMENT
Seattle, Washington
Completed: 2001

BIRD WATCHERS' HOUSE
Maple Valley, Washington
Completed: 2002

LATIN ZEN APARTMENT
Miami, Florida
Completed: 2002

BEAR PARK RESIDENCE, NORTHWEST FAMILY RETREAT
(With Scott Allen)
Bellevue, Washington
Completed: 2002

RESIDENCE
(With Scott Allen)
Bainbridge Island, Washington
Completed: 2003

OCEAN HOUSE
Island of Hawaii, Hawaii
Completed: 2003

HANSON RESIDENCE REMODEL
Seattle, Washington
Completed: 2003; unbuilt

LONGBRANCH CABIN ADDITION
Longbranch, Washington
Completed: 2003

FURNITURE DESIGN, LONGBRANCH CABIN ADDITION
Longbranch, Washington
Completed: 2003

RESIDENCE REMODEL
Medina, Washington
Completed: 2003

LAKE HOUSE
Mercer Island, Washington
Completed: 2003

FURNITURE DESIGN, LAKE HOUSE
Mercer Island, Washington
Completed: 2004

MODERN ANTEBELLUM HOUSE
Atlanta, Georgia
Completed: 2004

AN AMERICAN PLACE
Hunts Point, Washington
Completed: 2004

HOUSE OF LIGHT
Medina, Washington
Completed: 2005

RESIDENCE REMODEL
Mercer Island, Washington
Completed: 2005

LAKE MINNETONKA RESIDENCE
Wayzata, Minnesota
Completed: 2005

CONDOMINIUM
Seattle, Washington
Completed: 2005

RESIDENCE REMODEL
Orcas Island, Washington
Completed: 2006

SHOW LOW RESIDENCE
Show Low, Arizona
Completed: 2006

RESIDENCE
Napa, California
Completed: 2006; unbuilt

RESIDENCE
Seattle, Washington
Completed: 2006

TRANSPARENT LOFT
Seattle, Washington
Completed: 2007

PORTLAND CONDOMINIUM
Portland, Oregon
Completed: 2007

**NOAH'S ARK AT THE
SKIRBALL CULTURAL CENTER**
(With Alan Maskin)
Los Angeles, California
Completed: 2007

CITY APARTMENT
Seattle, Washington
Completed: 2007

HAHN HILL
Yakima, Washington
Completed: 2007; unbuilt

VILLA JUMEIRAH PROJECT
United Arab Emirates
Completed: 2007; unbuilt

HAWAIIAN RESIDENCE
Island of Hawaii, Hawaii
Completed: 2007; unbuilt

ART COLLECTOR'S LOFT
Seattle, Washington
Completed: 2007

RESIDENCE
Calabasas, California
Completed: 2007; unbuilt

BORREGO SPRINGS RESIDENCE REMODEL
San Diego County, California
Completed: 2008

HONG KONG VILLA
Hong Kong, China
Completed: 2008

**FURNITURE DESIGN,
HONG KONG VILLA**
Hong Kong, China
Completed: 2008

GLASS FARMHOUSE
Eastern Oregon
Completed: 2008

DECORATIVE ARTS HOUSE
Denver, Colorado
Completed: 2008

**FURNITURE DESIGN,
DECORATIVE ARTS HOUSE**
Denver, Colorado
Completed: 2008

GLASS APARTMENT REMODEL
Seattle, Washington
Completed: 2008

**FURNITURE DESIGN,
GLASS APARTMENT REMODEL**
Seattle, Washington
Completed: 2008

CAPITAL HOUSE
Washington, D.C.
Completed: 2008

PANGYO NEW CITY PROJECT
Seoul, Republic of Korea
Completed: 2008; unbuilt

**LIGHTCATCHER AT THE
WHATCOM MUSEUM**
Bellingham, Washington
Completed: 2009

URBAN YOGA SPA
Seattle, Washington
Completed: 2009

2010s

HONG KONG TOY COMPANY
Hong Kong, China
Phases completed: 2010, 2014

MEXICO BEACH HOUSE
San José del Cabo, Baja, Mexico
Completed: 2010

NORTHWOODS HOUSE
Iron River, Michigan
Completed: 2010

FURNITURE DESIGN, NORTHWOODS HOUSE
Iron River, Michigan
Completed: 2010

THE PEAK HOUSE
Hong Kong, China
Completed: 2010; unbuilt

RESIDENCE
Seoul, Republic of Korea
Completed: 2011

"JIM OLSON: ARCHITECTURE FOR ART" EXHIBIT, MUSEUM OF ART WASHINGTON STATE UNIVERSITY
Pullman, Washington
Completed: 2011

PAVILION HOUSE
Bellevue, Washington
Completed: 2011

RESIDENCE PROJECT
Hong Kong, China
Completed: 2011; unbuilt

JAPANESE AMERICAN NATIONAL MUSEUM
Los Angeles, California
Completed: 2011; unbuilt

CABIN
Port Ludlow, Washington
Completed: in progress

STUBBS ROAD
Hong Kong, China
Completed: 2011; unbuilt

RESIDENCE REMODEL
Hayden Lake, Idaho
Completed: 2012

RESIDENCE REMODEL
Seattle, Washington
Completed: 2012

RESIDENCE REMODEL
Seattle, Washington
Completed: 2012

SEOUL SHOPS
Seoul, Republic of Korea
Completed: 2012

COTTAGE REMODEL
Longbranch, Washington
Completed: 2012

GETHSEMANE CHAPEL
Seattle, Washington
Completed: 2012

COUNTRY GARDEN HOUSE
Portland, Oregon
Completed: 2013

CHRISTIAN SCIENCE READING ROOM
Seattle, Washington
Completed: 2013

**"JIM OLSON: ART IN ARCHITECTURE"
EXHIBIT, THE WHATCOM MUSEUM**
Bellingham, Washington
Completed: 2013

CLIFF DWELLING
White Rock, British Columbia, Canada
Completed: 2013

SHANGHAI PENTHOUSE PROJECT
Shanghai, China
Completed: 2013

"JIM OLSON" EXHIBIT, RAINIER CLUB
Seattle, Washington
Completed: 2013

RESIDENCE
Los Angeles, California
Completed: 2013; unbuilt

**BELLEVUE BOTANICAL GARDEN
VISITOR CENTER**
Bellevue, Washington
Completed: 2014

**"OLSON KUNDIG: ANTHOLOGY"
KANEKO EXHIBIT**
Omaha, Nebraska
Completed: 2014

RESIDENCE
Houston, Texas
Completed: 2014; unbuilt

BLAKELY ISLAND ART STUDIO
Blakely Island, Washington
Completed: 2014

HAVEN OF REFLECTION
Seattle, Washington
Completed: 2014

LUGANO APARTMENT
Lugano, Switzerland
Completed: 2014

HARBOR LOFT CONDOMINIUM
Seattle, Washington
Completed: 2014

LONGBRANCH CABIN ADDITION
Longbranch, Washington
Completed: 2014

FOX ISLAND RESIDENCE
Fox Island, Washington
Completed: 2014

**"JIM OLSON: HOME BASE" EXHIBIT,
COLLEGE OF BUILT ENVIRONMENTS
UNIVERSITY OF WASHINGTON**
Seattle, Washington
Completed: 2015

NORTHWEST ART HOUSE
Seattle, Washington
Completed: 2015

**FURNITURE DESIGN,
NORTHWEST ART HOUSE**
Seattle, Washington
Completed: 2015

RESIDENCE REMODEL
Omaha, Nebraska
Completed: 2015

CITY CABIN
Seattle, Washington
Completed: 2015

FOSS WATERWAY SEAPORT
(With Alan Maskin)
Tacoma, Washington
Completed: 2015

**BASECAMP, THE COLLECTORS LOUNGE
AT THE SEATTLE ART FAIR**
Seattle, Washington
Completed: 2015

**JW MARRIOTT LOS CABOS BEACH
RESORT AND SPA**
Puerto Los Cabos, Baja, Mexico
Completed: 2015

BAY AREA HILL HOUSE
San Francisco Bay Area, California
Completed: 2015

RESIDENCE REMODEL
Medina, Washington
Completed: 2015

RESIDENCE REMODEL
Seattle, Washington
Completed: 2016; unbuilt

RESIDENCE
Newport Beach, California
Completed: 2016; unbuilt

TAIWAN VILLAS
Taipei, Taiwan
Completed: 2016

TOFINO BEACH HOUSE
Tofino, British Columbia, Canada
Completed: 2016

**FURNITURE DESIGN,
TOFINO BEACH HOUSE**
Tofino, British Columbia, Canada
Completed: 2016

BUILDING PROJECT
Seattle, Washington
Completed: 2016; unbuilt

RAINIER VISTA RESIDENCE
Seattle, Washington
Completed: 2016; unbuilt

HUDSON VALLEY RESIDENCE
Westchester, New York
Completed: 2017

CALIFORNIA MEADOW HOUSE
Woodside, California
Completed: 2017

**KIRKLAND MUSEUM OF FINE
& DECORATIVE ART**
Denver, Colorado
Completed: in progress

TRAIN STATION, HOTEL, AND MARKET
California
Completed: in progress

LOVELAND MUSEUM/GALLERY
(With Kirsten Murray)
Loveland, Colorado
Completed: in progress

RESIDENCE
Santa Cruz, California
Completed: in progress

RESIDENCE REMODEL
Seattle, Washington
Completed: in progress

FLOATING HOME
Seattle, Washington
Completed: in progress

**JORDAN SCHNITZER MUSEUM OF ART,
WASHINGTON STATE UNIVERSITY**
Pullman, Washington
Completed: in progress

RESIDENCE REMODEL
California
Completed: in progress

RESIDENCE
Seoul, Republic of Korea
Completed: in progress

CITY GARDEN RESIDENCE
Indonesia
Completed: in progress

RESIDENCE
(With Kevin M. Kudo-King)
Los Angeles, California
Completed: in progress

RESIDENCE
United Kingdom
Completed: in progress

ST. MARK'S CATHEDRAL, EAST FAÇADE
Seattle, Washington
Completed: in progress

PORTLAND ESTATE ADDITION
Portland, Oregon
Completed: in progress

ORCHARD HOUSE
Kirkland, Washington
Completed: in progress

COSTA RICA RESIDENCE
(With Kevin M. Kudo-King)
Costa Rica
Completed: in progress

JACKSON SQUARE GALLERY
Completed: in progress

URBAN RESIDENCE
India
Completed: in progress

ACKNOWLEDGMENTS

First of all, I want to thank my beautiful wife of 47 years, Katherine, for her love, encouragement and patience. She has been with me through almost all of my career and without her steady moral support, my career could not have happened.

I want to thank my clients who have trusted me to take them on a journey into the unknown. Their faith in me led to the results we achieved together. Thanks also to the contractors, craftspeople, and artists who made our dreams into reality and in many cases, made the outcome even richer than we had imagined. I owe a very special thanks to Chris Burnside and MacKenzie Cotters. Their talents and ceaseless dedication have made this book what it is. It would not have happened without them. Thanks to Evan Harlan and Tessa Crespo for the beautiful plans in this book. These drawings make the book one of a kind. Thanks also to Gabriela Frank, Ciara Cronin, Lauren Gallow, and Stephanie Pieper. I want to thank Jerry Garcia, who offered helpful insights and advice throughout the process. Another special thanks goes to archivist Laura Grove, who tirelessly rediscovered all the information in the chronology. Working with her was a satisfying and cathartic experience for me—going through my professional and artistic past in great detail. I want to thank Aaron Betsky for his perceptive insights into my work and his eloquent writing. I learned more from Aaron than I had ever imagined. Thanks to Lucas Dietrich and Fleur Jones of Thames & Hudson for listening to our stories, looking at our images, and turning it into a book that, to me, perfectly represents my philosophy.

OLSON KUNDIG, 1966–

Architecture is a group effort. For me, it is like a marathon – a long race where we cross the finish line together, and one that is both challenging and rewarding along the way.

I dedicate this book to the many people who run this marathon alongside me. To my amazing partners – Tom, Kirsten, Alan and Kevin – who are good friends and a great inspiration to me. I am so fortunate to have them by my side. To the talented, dedicated members of our firm, now and for the past 50 years, who have contributed to our work in countless ways, day after day, year after year. As the saying goes, "If you want to go fast, go alone. If you want to go far, go together."

We want to go far.

Kit Cheung, Lauren Small, Phil Turner, Briony Walker, Kaz Murata, Justin Hazelwood, Cameron Shampine, Maria Do, Amanda Cruser, Catherine Popolow, Derek Pirozzi, Kevin Kluender, Joe Iano, Athanasios Ikonomou, Gordon Fleener, Joshua Frank, Steve Schlenker, Dejan Miovic, Marina Komkov, Lane Williams, Krishna Bharathi, Justin Dennis, Paul Irving, Spencer Fornaciari, Brandon Crain, Peter Hanby, Maximillian Foley, Kathleen Monda, Lori Jo Tanaka, Henry Pierce, John Mrozek, Dan Caine, Debbie Kennedy, Jiahui Wang, Jason Frantzen, Benoit-Noe Chaste, Kirsten Murray, Stefan Wong, Paula Calderon, Christina Kilday, David Cinamon, Ryann Brady, Douglas Farrell, Samantha Gutteridge, Susan Thorne, Violeta Ebreo, Melinda Ekin, Jane Buck, Andrew Ellis, William Morris, Susan Dang, Kalee Mutch, Kirsten Akerman, Megan Zimmerman, Kyle Gwilt, Susan Palermo, Matthias Winkler, Yue Chen, Yasuko Tarumi, Henry Antupit, Phillip Bahar, Leah Martin, John Hallock, Barbara Swierc, Alysia Lund, Shu Fang Chou, Jacob Schell, Norman Millar, Julie Riegel, Jennifer Heinfeld, Mariana Gutheim, Kathryn Nelson, Pete Austin, Grant Gustafson, Noreen Shinohara, Tim Carlander, Anthony DeJesus, Cima Malek-Aslani, Adam Garrett, Denise Tomlinson, Tiago Trigo, Nahoko Ueda, David Shannon, Chad Harding, Steven Taylor, Laura Sinn, Katie Miller, Francesca Krisli, Dawn McConaghy, Patricia Chambers, Stephen Grim, Margaret Gaul, Jonathan Walston, Steven Peters, Pat Anderson, Dennis Yu, Benjamin Hall, Adam Davidson, Steven Rainville, Shea Bajaj, Daniel Shumaker, Ryan Stephenson, Kim Lokan, Nannette Manson, Jason Imani, Jim Graham, Abhishek Bawiskar, Peggy Zafarana,

Claire Fontaine, Thomas Schatte, Phil Graham, Elizabeth Conklin, Robert Raasch, Eric Druse, Trevor Dykstra, Francisca Valenzuela, Tara Cahn, Lauren Tatusko, Rich Murakami, Johnathan Agnes, Ming-Lee Yuan, Gordon Lynch, Kanog-Anong Nimakorn, Jatinder Gill, Jeffrey Ocampo, Gavin Argo, Allan Nunez, Tim Rohleder, William Caramella, Maxwell Schnutgen, Jordan Leppert, Cecilia Chavez, Laura Senie, Ekram Hassen, Bryce Tolene, Kelly Schnieders, Doan Nhi, Campie Drobnack, Gregory Nakata, Cory Crocker, Simon Clews, Christopher Gerrick, Bob Wagoner, Sini Kamppari-Pearson, Zachary Stevens, Benjamin Anderson-Nelson, Eider Garcia, Andrea Romheld, Breanna Millett Cabais, Varun Thautam, Stacey Upton, Walter Schacht, Rick Ghillino, Christine Burkland, Alex Fritz, Hayden Robinson, Joyce Larson, Brianna Schoeneman, Johnathon Smith, Marla Simpson, MacKenzie Cotters, Finn Charleson, Karl Schmidt, Emily Maxey, Julia Khorsand, Robert Jakubik, Scott Allen, Breck Craparo, Lang Wang, Samuel Irons, Traci Skov, Serene Wongsa, Marcy Shaw, William Mooreston, Jesse Chappelle, Paul Schlachter, Kathryn Rogers, Myat Htoo Aung, Reed Kelly, Renee Boone, Michael Wagner, Greg Lewis, William Kemper, Clay Anderson, Kristen Becker, Mindy Gudzinski, Roberto Ramirez, Rina Chinen, Todd Waffner, Anjali Grant, Mark Keller, Christopher Butler, Ernest Wang, Angela Ray, Earl Edwards, Taehyung Kim, Angus MacGregor, Chironne Moller, Jarri Hasnain, Tyler Myers, Mike Yoshihara, Jon Gentry, Nils Finne, Jia Dong, Kyle Barker, Floyd Grant, Mikel Amias, Ratna Laksana, Kevin Scott, Stephanus Prabawa, Matthew Hostetler, TJ Tuey, Aimee O'Carroll, Jim Conti, Amy Koenig, Abigail Archer, David Fuchs, Evan Harlan, Mark Snyder, Werner Stoll, Phoebe Fornaciari, Dong Uk Kim, Crystal Coleman, Kahn Kuo, Les Eerkes, Gladys Ly-AuYoung, Casey Hill, John Kennedy, Katherine Knutson, Susan Luke, Irina Bokova, Maresa Patterson, Phil Beck, John Riordan, Noah Conlay, Jonathan Junker, Randy Everett, Rebecca Moore, Jim Friesz, Tracy Margel, Serena Gardiner, Thomas Brown, Mark Richardson, Curtis Eppley, Kelly Brooks, David Day, Colleen Redfield, Ryan Patterson, Wesley Hsi, Daniel Renner, Drew Chapman, Benjamin Dimmitt, Jon Decker, Rick Sundberg, Jim Cutler, Brent Pfister, Valerie Wersinger, Carsten Stinn, Megan Carter, Mark Mappala, Jamie Slagel, Todd Matthes, Stephen Yamada-Heidner, Marc Tegen, Robert Baur, William Franklin, Christian Ruud, Corey Collier, Kelsey Rudd, Johanna Reed, Samuel Gibson, Kimberly Shoemake-Medlock, Marlene Chen, Stephen Quenell, Anna Sabine Rose, Steven Wojtynek, Kaoru Schorn, Matt Aalfs, Hunter Van Bramer, Daichi Yamaguchi, Michael Gore, Molly Evans, Britton Shepard, Aaron Fein, Alix Ogilvie, Sarah Muchow, Victor Badami II, John Nebendahl, Katerina Leung, Anna Sabine Rose, Tony Kim, Michael Stevens, Sora Key, Song An, Sofia Poe, Margaret Undine, Christian Poules, Mark Wettstone, Kenny Wilson, Joshua Brevoort, Heather Cooper, Taisuke Ikegami, Ana Brainard, Michael Mekonen, Janice Wettstone, Cornelia Herger, Adam Pearce, Dick Dunbar, Jorge Ribera, Derek Santo, Connor Dinnison, Rehanna Rojiani, Bjoern Kastrup, Lauren Gallow, Daniel Ralls, Sarah Kia, Silvia Miralles, Gordon Walker, Megan Adams, Matthew Stannard, Andrew vanLeewen, John Outterson, Shelley Forge, Kyle Griesmeyer, Rik Adams, Ting Zhang, Timothy Politis, Kiron Cheema, Brian Walters, Katrina Morgan, Alexander Bremer, Sormeh Azad, Lila Wengler, Dong Uk Kim, Danielle Quenell, Kelly Smolenski, Colin Ostman, Leslie Ann Brown, Donald Boothby, Shu Hui Chang, Edward U, Fergus Knox, Adam Monkaba, Andrew Thies, Michele Darling, Donna Kovelenko, Pleumjit Chaiya, Grace Schlitt, Bent Geinitz, Martina Bendel, Rohit Eustace, Noah Wadden, Derek Ryder, Michelle Coetzee, Blake Williams, A Rum Cho, Christelle Coetzee, Tri Ly, Zivko Penzar, Jay Coupard, Eric Neuhaus, Louis Cody Lodi, Dan Wilson, Jens Christensen, Adam Pazan, Louis Cody Lodi, Susan Boyle, Curtis James Christensen, Marco Chimienti, Huyen Hoang, Christine Pedersen, Jane Devine, Luke Wendler, Gabriela Denise Frank, Thomas Sheridan, Betty Huang, Yara Machado, Bill Hook, Bradley Conway, Brandon Olin, Monica Le, Jim Olson, Shu Fang Chou, Dain Susman, Rick Mohler, Teresa Sinnett, Kilian Ruggiero-Upton, Christian Crisologo, Steve Kern, Tina Song, Jeffrey Busby, Suzanne Stefan, Kaleigh Young, Naomi Mason, Cailen Pybus, James Goodspeed, Emily Schaefer, Holly Simon, Won Sik Lee, Ryan Nace, Nancy Haugen, Jayson Kabala, Kee Song, Cambria Silva de Jesus, Marc Furst, Ariel Kemp, Sheri Locke, Edward Lalonde, Amir Ghazanfari, ChiaLin Ma, Lesley McTague, Michael Picard, Nicola Chan, Brooks Cavender, Tim Rholeden, Andres Moguel, Matthew Empson, Matthew Weighall, Dawn Bushnaq, Patti Wilma, Nathan Boyd, Birgit Wollgast, Serhan Tekbas, Matthew Weiss, Joanne Graney, Rick Adams, Steve Saude, Marc Brown, Michelle Arab, Chen Xia, Andreas Wiebe, Fikerte Befekadu, Ida Polzer, Alan Maskin, Lori Kirsis, Zachary George, Charles Shugart, Teri Sinnett, Kathy Hanway, Andrew Enright, Plamena Milusheva, Sondra Schneberger, Noah Winkler, Tiffany Twardzik, Megan Quinn, Marnie Pardee, Romail Dhaddey, James Gilman, Leann Crist, Shawn Kemna, Tessa Crespo, Evan Dobson, Dakotah Apostolou, Yuki Seda-Kane, Jody Carroll, Atsuko Mori, Jerry Garcia, Brett Baba, Wing-Yee Leung-Wilson, Supatra Huangyutitham, Kevin Bineham, Nathan Petty, Rachel Klein, Darren Murrey, Shu Hui Chang, Dayo Jones, Sky Lanigan-Durchslag, Maureen Salisbury, Jesse Kingsley, Dennis Mortensen, Rebecca Brown, Cristina Acevedo, Mike Winnick, Jason Mais, Rune Martinson, Matt Anderson, Nicholas Johnson, Roger Hilbert, Sarah Long, Blair Payson, Stephanie Pieper, Richard Hu, Zoe Friedman Melendez, Steve Carlton, Ryan Botts, Peter Wilson, Kasia Glamowska, Michael Goldman, Margot Smith, James Butler, Jona Bartell, Gordon Metzger, Sheena Garcia, Michelle Hamilton, Robert Drucker, Maria Singer, Robert Lee, David Burya, Shane Lowe, Merritt Palminteri, Lee Braun, Chee Sandra Choy, Tony Case, Edward Wilson,

Brooks Brainerd, Daniel Temple, Johanna Schorr, Lindsay Kunz, Tomomi Yashiro, Andy Kiu On Lai, Susan Stump, Ryan Tretow, Chris Burnside, Jill Saidyan, Rachel Ravitz, William Preston, Alexi Paparo, Ciara Cronin, Jason Roseler, Kristi Larson, Robert Horner, Mark Demko, Slava Simontov, Devant Asawla, Ian Carr, Michelle Han, Kelly Sommerfeld, David Yarza, Tim Gudgel, Stephen Wood, Vikram Sami, Kozo Nozawa, John Thomas, Chinatsu Thompson, John Savo, Elisa Renouard, Justin Helmbrecht, Samuel Tannenbaum, Alexander Pfeiffer, Piper Carafa-Olson, Carey Moran, Connor Irick, Kevin Driscoll, Laura Bartunek, Lavon Gomes, Scott Viloria, Taina Karr, Joseph Filippelli, Tara Edwards, John Woollen, Kevin Spence, Brian Jonas, Jason Mass, Olivier Landa, Mona Davey, Alice Boytz, Corey DiRutigliano, Amelia Harrington, Raquel Mayorga, Bryan Berkas, Marilyn Jarrell, Sung Cho, Sapna Patel, Won Sik Lee, Regina Muenstermann, Amanda Chenoweth, Brent Rogers, Sarah Haubner, Jennifer Bohan, Michelle Nolte, Shannon Denton, Meagan Palmer, Stacy Rowland, Steven Carpenter, Mira-Yui Mui, Annelise Aldrich, Lora Hammersmith, Jeff Witzel, Samuel Sze, Matt Melcher, John Vierra, Dennis Alkier, Sane Nobles, Martha Rogers, Laina Navarro, Mark Olthoff, Isabel Hankart, Matthew Kent, Jacqualyn Adelstein, James Smith, Patricia Flores, Erin Hamilton, Kyle Phillips, Millie Reinhardsen, Robert Poules, Katherine Ranieri, Alicia Requena Carrion, James Steel, Michael Rogers, Nick Lathum, Brian Lee, Adam Longenbach, Kendra Lundahl, Min Cho, Alivia Owens, Charlie Hellstern, Stephanie Bower, Nicholas McDaniel, Bin Yu, Rob Nevitt, Crisanna Siegert, Juan Ferreira, Steve Sivak, Laura Ellen Cecil, Kristien Ruggiero-Upton, Jerome Tryon, Armin Quilici, Bill Booth, Ramona Page, Chee San Sandra Choy, Jeroen Bomers, James Juricevich, Amanda Darling, Richard Sachs, Sarah Smith, Bill Sleeth, Max Bemberg, Tim Bies, Garin Schenk, Erica Williams, Drew Shawver, Wei Yan, Terry Walker, Steve Bourne, Garreth Schuh, Anthony Ngo, Francesco Crocenzi, Sarah Mann, Benjamin Kruse, Martha Weiss, Misun Chung Gerrick, Theresa Van Ert, Kevin Kudo-King, Michael Wright, Juliet Sinisterra Cole, Suzanne Zahr, Tod Heisteman, Jesse Nickerson, Felix Cheong, Marian Maestretti, Aaron Schmidt, Tom Kundig, Cale Wilber, William Jackson, Chenxi Gong, Yousman Okano, Roma Shah, Motomi Kudo-King, Sasha Leon, Ellen Southard, Damandeep Khatra, Terry Findeisen, Peter Brunner, Mallory Fair, Ilka Gronert, Kevin Barden, Katharine Van Anda, Nicole Hester

AUTHOR BIOGRAPHIES

Jim Olson has been designing buildings and spaces that explore the aesthetic interplay of art, nature, and architecture for over fifty years. Founding partner of Olson Kundig, the Seattle-based architect is best known for his houses, particularly for art collectors, though his interest in exploring the relationship between light and space also extends to his large-scale projects including museums, religious spaces, and commercial buildings. Now spanning thirteen countries and four continents, each of Olson's projects is carefully calibrated to site and client. From the beginning, his aim has been for architecture to support and frame its surroundings, rather than stand apart from it. Whether a cabin on the shores of Puget Sound, a 14-acre (6-hectare) luxury resort in Baja, Mexico, or a fine art museum in downtown Denver, Olson's architecture encourages people to focus their attention on the inherent beauty of what is around them.

Often described as "warm modernism," Olson's elegant and refined architecture is softened through his use of natural materials and careful crafting of light. His work finds a balance between monumentality and intimacy, drawing inspiration from sources as broad as the temples of ancient Egypt to the simplicity of a bird's nest or a single flower in a forest. The Northwest—its climate and dramatic landscape, where one can live outside two-thirds of the year—has been a strong influence on Olson since his childhood. It informs his deep sensitivity to nature, resulting in buildings that weave into their surroundings as if they had always been there. Taken together, Olson's body of work expresses the power of contextual design: architecture that fits into its cultural, built and natural environments in a way that makes for a better whole.

Aaron Betsky is dean of the Frank Lloyd Wright School of Architecture and a former practitioner, critic, curator, and museum director. He has been deeply engaged with the world of architecture for almost fifty years and is the author of numerous monographs.

PROJECT CREDITS

CAPITAL HOUSE
Washington, D.C., USA
2008

Project Team:
Jim Olson – Design Principal
Kevin Kudo-King – Project Manager
Ming Yuan – Project Architect
Michael Wright – Architectural Staff
Chad Harding – Architectural Staff
Trevor Dykstra – Architectural Staff
Kevin Scott – Architectural Staff
Christine Burkland – Interior Design
Charlie Hellstern – Interior Design
Cristina Acevedo – Interior Design

Contributors:
Brian Hood Lighting Design, Inc. – Lighting Designer
Lifecraft, Inc. – General Contractor
MCE Structural Consultants – Structural Engineer
Robertson D. Witmer – Civil Engineer
Stephen Stimson Associates, Landscape Architects, Inc. – Landscape Architects
Tuazon Engineering – Consultant

LIGHTCATCHER AT THE WHATCOM MUSEUM
Bellingham, Washington, USA
2009

Project Team:
Jim Olson – Design Principal
Alan Maskin – Principal
Stephen Yamada-Heidner – Project Manager
John Kennedy – Project Architect
Olivier Landa – Construction Administration Manager
William Franklin – Architectural Staff
Megan Zimmerman – Architectural Staff
Michael Picard – Architectural Staff
Cristina Acevedo – Interior Design

Contributors:
Abacus – Mechanical Engineers
Candela – Lighting Designer
Charles Anderson Landscape Architecture, Inc. – Landscape Architecture
David Nelson & Associates, LLC – LEED Consultant
Ebenal General – General Contractor
Eskilsson Architecture – Specifications
Magnusson Klemencic Associates – Structural Engineer
Sparling, Inc. – Electrical Engineer
Wilson Engineering, LLC – Civil Engineer

MEXICO BEACH HOUSE
San José del Cabo, Baja, Mexico
2010

Project Team:
Jim Olson – Design Principal
Bob Jakubik – Project Manager
Jason Roseler – Project Architect
Janice Wettstone – Architectural Staff
Derek Santo – Architectural Staff
Daniel Ralls – Architectural Staff
Christine Burkland – Interior Design

Contributors:
Constructora Malver – General Contractor
dePelecyn Studio – Lighting Designer
E Group – Landscape Architect
MCE Structural Consultants, Inc. – Structural Engineer
Stantec Consulting Services – Mechanical Engineer
Terry Hunziker – Interior Design

NORTHWOODS HOUSE
Iron River, Michigan, USA
2010

Project Team:
Jim Olson – Design Principal
Olivier Landa – Project Manager
Brett Baba – Project Manager
Michael Wright – Project Architect
Jacqualyn Adelstein – Architectural Staff

Contributors:
Brian Hood Lighting Design, Inc. – Lighting Designer
MBM Construction Company – General Contractor
MCE Structural Consultants, Inc. – Structural Engineer
Riederer Engineering, LLC – Mechanical Engineer
Stephen Stimson Associates Landscape Architects, Inc. – Landscape Architect
STS Consultants, Ltd. – Civil Engineer

PAVILION HOUSE
Bellevue, Washington, USA
2011

Project Team:
Jim Olson – Design Principal
Les Eerkes – Project Manager
Steven Carpenter – Architectural Staff

Contributors:
Toth Construction, Inc. – General Contractor
Associated Earth Sciences, Inc. – Civil Engineer
MCE Structural Consultants, Inc. – Structural Engineer
Franklin Engineering – Mechanical Engineer
Garret Cord Werner, LLC – Interior Design
Charles Anderson Landscape Architecture, Inc. – Landscape Architect
Brian Hood Lighting Design, Inc. – Lighting Designer
The Watershed Company – Consultant

SEOUL SHOPS
Seoul, South Korea
2012

Project Team:
Jim Olson – Design Principal
William Franklin – Project Manager
John Nebendahl – Architectural Staff

Contributors:
Moonbeam Lighting – Lighting Designer
Studio 216 Inc. – Consultant

GETHSEMANE CHAPEL
Seattle, Washington, USA
2012

Project Team:
Jim Olson – Design Principal
Bob Jakubik – Project Manager
Nahoko Ueda – Architectural Staff
Megan Zimmerman – Architectural Staff
Jerry Garcia – Architectural Staff
Christine Burkland – Interior Design

Contributors:
Brian Hood Lighting Design, Inc. – Lighting Design
Candela – Lighting Designer
Cierra Electrical Group, Inc. – Electrical Engineer
Coughlin Porter Lundeen, Inc. – Civil and Structural Engineer
Peter David Studio, Inc. – Art Glass

Rafn Company – General Contractor
Sider + Byers Associates, Inc. – Mechanical Engineer
SMR Architects – Associate Architects
The Berger Partnership – Landscape Architect

COUNTRY GARDEN HOUSE
Portland, Oregon, USA
2013

Project Team:
Jim Olson – Design Principal
Stephen Grim – Project Manager
Martha Rogers – Project Architect
Bryan Berkas – Architectural Staff
Christine Burkland – Interior Design

Contributors:
Brian Hood Lighting Design, Inc. – Lighting Designer
Daniel J. Hinkley – Landscape Architect
Dynamic Architectural Windows and Doors – Consultant
Madden & Baughman Engineering, Inc. – Structural Engineer
Otis Construction, Inc. – General Contractor
Spearhead – Consultant
ZTEC Engineers, Inc. – Civil Engineer

CLIFF DWELLING
White Rock, British Columbia, Canada
2013

Project Team:
Jim Olson – Design Principal
Elizabeth Bianchi Conklin – Project Manager
Megan Quinn – Project Architect
Misun Gerrick – Architectural Staff

Contributors:
Brian Hood Lighting Design, Inc. – Lighting Designer
Highliner Construction, Ltd. – General Contractor
PCS Structural Solutions – Structural Engineer
Schmidt Bros Plumbing and Heating, Ltd. – Mechanical Engineer

BELLEVUE BOTANICAL GARDEN VISITOR CENTER
Bellevue, Washington, USA
2014

Project Team:
Jim Olson – Design Principal
Kevin Kudo-King – Principal
Martina Bendel – Project Manager
Misun Gerrick – Project Architect
Renee Boone – Architectural Staff

Contributors:
Barbara Swift – Landscape Architect
Cornerstone General Contractors, Inc. – General Contractor
Dan Hinkley - Plantsman
KPFF Consulting Engineers – Structural Engineer
Magnusson Klemencic Associates – Civil Engineer
Tuazon Engineering – Consultant
WSP – Electrical Engineer
WSP Flack and Kurtz – Lighting Design

LONGBRANCH CABIN
Longbranch, Washington, USA
1959, 1981, 1997, 2003, 2014

1959 Project Team:
Jim Olson – Design Principal

1981 Project Team:
Jim Olson – Design Principal
Brent Rogers – Project Manager

Contributors:
Tom Harris – General Contractor

1997 Project Team:
Jim Olson – Design Principal
Steve Clark – General Contractor

2003 Project Team:
Jim Olson – Design Principal
Ellen Cecil – Project Manager
Derek Santo – Architectural Staff

Contributors:
Brian Hood Lighting Design – Lighting Designer
Mark Ambler – General Contractor
MCE Structural Consultants, Inc. – Structural Engineer

2014 Project Team:
Jim Olson – Design Principal
William Franklin – Project Manager
Charlie Hellstern – Interiors Project Manager

Contributors:
Brian Hood Lighting Design – Lighting Designer
Mark Ambler – General Contractor
MCE Structural Consultants, Inc. – Structural Engineer

BLAKELY ISLAND ART STUDIO
Blakely Island, Washington, USA
2014

Project Team:
Jim Olson – Design Principal
Mark Olthoff – Project Manager
Yousman Okano – Architectural Staff
Gus Lynch – Architectural Staff

Contributors:
Needham Construction – General Contractor
MCE Structural Consultants, Inc. – Structural Engineer

HAVEN OF REFLECTION
Seattle, Washington, USA
2014

Project Team:
Jim Olson – Design Principal
Naomi Mason – Interior Design Manager
Elisa Renouard – Architectural Staff
Irina Bokova – Interior Design

Contributors:
12th Avenue Iron, Inc. – Custom fabricator
Brian Hood Lighting Design, Inc. – Lighting Designer
Schultz Miller, Inc. – General Contractor
Village Interiors, Inc. – Custom furniture fabricator

HONG KONG TOY COMPANY
Hong Kong, China
2010, 2014

Project Team:
Jim Olson – Design Principal
William Franklin – Project Manager
Martina Bendel – Architectural Staff
Charlie Hellstern – Interior Design
Cristina Acevedo – Interior Design
Irina Bokova – Interior Design

Contributors:
Brainfield Limited – General Contractor
Tino Kwan – Lighting Designer

FOX ISLAND RESIDENCE
Fox Island, Washington, USA
2014

Project Team:
Jim Olson – Design Principal
William Franklin – Project Manager
Christine Burkland – Interior Design

Contributors:
Bykonen Carter Quinn – Structural Engineer
Moonbeam Lighting – Lighting Designer
Schuchart Dow – General Contractor

CITY CABIN
Seattle, Washington, USA
2015

Project Team:
Jim Olson – Design Principal
Renee Boone – Project Manager/Project Architect
Christine Burkland – Interior Design

Contributors:
Brandon Peterson (The Palm Room) – Landscape Architect
dePelecyn Studio – Lighting Designer
Dovetail General Contractors – General Contractor
MCE Structural Consultants, Inc. – Structural Engineer

FOSS WATERWAY SEAPORT
Tacoma, Washington, USA
2015

Project Team:
Jim Olson – Design Principal
Alan Maskin – Principal, Exhibit Design
Jim Friesz – Project Manager
Bryan Berkas – Project Architect
Kevin Scott – Renderings

Contributors:
Jones and Roberts Company – General Contractor
KPFF Consulting Engineers – Structural Engineer
Luma Lighting Design – Lighting Designer
PAE Consulting Engineers Inc. – Mechanical/Electrical Engineer

JW MARRIOTT LOS CABOS BEACH RESORT AND SPA
Puerto Los Cabos, Baja, Mexico
2015

Project Team:
Jim Olson – Design Principal
Kevin Kudo-King – Principal
Jerry Garcia – Project Manager
Martina Bendel – Architectural Staff
Jorge Ribera – Architectural Staff
Cristina Acevedo – Interior Design
Debbie Kennedy – Interior Design
Charlie Hellstern – Interior Design

Contributors:
Alonso & Associados, Inc. – Structural Engineer
Grupo Diestra – General Contractor
Idea Asociados de Mexico – Executive Architect
Luz En Arquitectura SC – Lighting Design
Michelle Arab Studio – Landscape Architect

NORTHWEST ART HOUSE
Seattle, Washington, USA
2015

Project Team:
Jim Olson – Design Principal
William Franklin – Project Manager/Project Architect
Naho Ukeda – Architectural Staff
Crystal Coleman – Architectural Staff
Charlie Hellstern – Interior Design

Contributors:
Allworth Design P.S. – Landscape Architect
Brian Hood Lighting Design – Lighting Designer
Bykonen Carter Quinn – Structural Engineer
Coughlin Porter Lundeen, Inc. – Civil Engineer
Franklin Engineering – Mechanical Engineer
Jerry Fulks – Owner's Representative
Schultz Miller, Inc. – Contractor

BAY AREA HILL HOUSE
San Francisco Bay Area, California, USA
2015

Project Team:
Jim Olson – Design Principal
Bob Jakubik – Project Manager
Daniel Ralls – Project Architect
Michelle Hamilton – Architectural Staff
Martha Rogers – Architectural Staff
Crystal Coleman – Architectural Staff
Michael Wright – Architectural Staff
Ming Yuan – Architectural Staff
Debbie Kennedy – Interior Design Manager
Laina Navarro – Interior Design
Brianna Schoeneman – Interior Design
Rebecca Moore – Interior Design

Contributors:
Brian Hood Lighting Design, Inc. – Lighting Designer
CSW/ST 2 Engineering Group, Inc. – Civil Engineer
General Contractor – Kelly Pacific Construction and Thompson Brooks
Neumann Sloat Arnold Architects LLP – Building Envelope
PCS Structural Solutions – Structural Engineer
Stantec Consulting Services, Inc. – Mechanical Engineer
Surface Design, Inc. – Landscape Architect

TAIWAN VILLAS
Taipei, Taiwan
2016

Project Team:
Jim Olson – Design Principal
Kevin Kudo-King – Principal
Dan Wilson – Project Manager
Michael Wright –Architectural Staff
Jeff Ocampo – Architectural Staff
Andrew Ellis – Architectural Staff
Jorge Ribera – Architectural Staff
Chee San Sandra Choy – Architectural Staff
Peter Brunner – Architectural Staff
Rohit Eustace – Architectural Staff
Yuki Seda-Kane – Architectural Staff
Michael Picard – Architectural Staff
CJ Christensen – Architectural Staff
Simon Clews – Architectural Staff
Wing-Yee Leung-Wilson – Architectural Staff
Michelle Hamilton – Architectural Staff
Christine Burkland – Interior Design

Contributors:
Grand Vision Development Limited
Phoenix Property Investors, Inc.

TOFINO BEACH HOUSE
Tofino, British Columbia, Canada
2016

Project Team:
Jim Olson – Design Principal
Les Eerkes – Principal

Olivier Landa – Project Manager
Will Kemper – Project Architect
Christine Burkland – Interior Design Manager

Contributors:
Arup Canada, Inc. – Structural Engineer
Atlas Meridian Glass Works, Inc. – Consultant
Brian Hood Lighting Design, Inc. – Lighting Designer
Lewkowich Engineering Associates, Ltd. – Consultant
RDH Building Sciences, Inc. – Building Envelope
Schuchart Dow – General Contractor
Spearhead Timberworks – Consultant

HUDSON VALLEY RESIDENCE
Westchester, New York, USA
2017

Project Team:
Jim Olson – Design Principal
William Franklin – Project Manager
CJ Christensen – Project Architect
Jerry Garcia – Architectural Staff
Michelle Hamilton – Architectural Staff

Contributors:
Altieri Sebor Wieber LLC – Mechanical Engineer
Atlantic State Development – Owner's Representative
Edmond Hollander Landscape Architects – Landscape Architect
Kellard Sessions Consulting – Civil Engineer
Prutting & Company – General Contractor
Richard J. Shaver – Lighting Designer
Silman – Structural Engineer

CALIFORNIA MEADOW HOUSE
Woodside, California, USA
2017

Project Team:
Jim Olson – Design Principal
Olivier Landa – Project Manager
Alivia Owens – Project Architect
Blair Payson – Project Architect
Angus MacGregor – Architectural Staff

Laura Bartunek – Architectural Staff
Christine Burkland - Interior Design

Contributors:
Barker Co. – Home Automation/AV
Barnett Company – General Contractor
Big Leaf – Custom Furniture Fabricator
BRC Acoustics & Audiovisual Design – Acoustic Engineer
Brian Hood Lighting Design – Lighting Designer
Cobalt Power Systems – Photovoltaics
Juin Ho – Custom Furniture Fabricator
MacLeod and Associates – Civil Engineer
Mayer Designs – Custom Furniture Fabricator
Neumann Sloat Blanco Architects LLP – Building Envelope Consultant
OB Williams – Custom Interior Casework
PCS Structural Solutions – Structural Engineer
Spearhead – Custom Interior Casework
Stefan Gulassa – Custom Furniture Fabricator
Surface Design – Landscape Architect
WSP – Mechanical Engineer

KIRKLAND MUSEUM OF FINE & DECORATIVE ART
Denver, Colorado, USA
In progress

Project Team:
Jim Olson – Design Principal
Kirsten R. Murray – Principal
Crystal Coleman – Project Manager
Bryan Berkas – Project Architect
Martha Rogers – Project Architect
Daniel Ralls – Project Architect
Motomi Kudo-King – Architectural Staff
Clay Anderson – Architectural Staff
Naomi Mason – Interior Design

Contributors:
Creative Civil Solutions – Civil Engineering
Hefferan Partnership, Inc. – Gallery Lighting Designer
KL&A, Inc. – Structural Engineer
Mascarenaz and Associates – Owner's Representative
MKK Consulting Engineers – Mechanical, Electrical, and Plumbing Consultant
Shaw Construction – General Contractor
Wenk Associates – Landscape Architect

PICTURE CREDITS

Every reasonable effort has been made to identify rightsholders. Any errors or omissions will be corrected in subsequent editions.

PHOTOGRAPHY: Cindy Anderson: 33 / **Farshid Assassi:** 303 / **Benjamin Benschneider:** 4–5, 31, 34, 52, 56, 58–59, 61–64, 76–77, 79–83, 88–89, 91–96, 112, 186–87, 190T, 190BL, 196–200, 202–03, 209, 212, 279TR–81, 283T, 305, 306, 306, 307, 308, 309, 310, 310, 310, 310, 311, 311, 313, 313, 314, 314, 305 / **Tim Bies:** 21, 28, 35, 36, 50–51, 54–55, 57R, 68BL, 276TL, 276 BR, 279, 279TL, 279BR, 302, 303, 304, 307, 307, 308, 309, 309, 309, 310, 311 / **Jeremy Bitterman:** 101–03, 105–07, 121–23, 125–29, 161–63, 311, 312, 313 / **Chris Burnside:** 94–96, 114–15, 190BL, 194–95, 276TR, 276CL, 276BL, 283B, 311 / **Dick Busher:** 18, 20, 25, 288, 290, 291, 291, 299 / **Eduardo Calderon:** 27, 30, 295, 296, 300, 303, 303, 303, 303, 305, 305 / **Francisco Estrada:** 189T / **Alex Fradkin:** 272–74, 270–71, 272, 274, 275T, 275BR / **Thomas Grady:** 312 / **Art Grice:** 25, 296 / **Richard Hildahl:** 2–3 / **Michael Jensen:** 17, 298 / **Courtesy of Kirkland Museum:** 275BL / **Nic Lehoux:** cover, 42–44, 46–49, 108–09, 111, 236–37, 239–49, 251–52, 254–56, 277T, 309, 314, 314 / **Aaron Leitz:** 148–50, 152, 168–69, 171–76, 178–79, 181, 210–11, 312, 313, 313 / **Karen Melvin:** 306 / **Matthew Millman:** 214–15, 217–22, 224–29, 261–63, 265–68, 270–71, 315, 314 / **Grant Mudford:** 307 / **Martien Mulder:** 189B, 193, 201, 204 / **Ngoc Minh Ngo:** 66–68, 70–71, 73–75, 310 / **Heidi Obzina Torrance:** 288 / **Jim Olson:** 13, 29, 139 / **Ryan Patterson:** 11, 40, 134–35, 138, 144–47, 164–65, 167, 230–31, 233–35, 313, 314 / **Erhard Pfeiffer:** 26, 276CR, 308, 309 / **Robert Pisano:** 296, 296 / **Richard Powers:** 312 / **Mary Randlett:** 22, 286 / **Kevin Scott:** 84–85, 87, 130–31, 133, 140–43, 145, 157–59, 161B, 182–83, 185, 279BL, 311, 312, 313, 313, 313 / **Rafael Soldi:** 39 / **Sam Van Fleet:** 299 / **Bruce Van Inwegen:** 26, 28, 299, 302, 302, 306 / **John Vaughn:** 24 / **Dominique Vorillon:** 32, 303 / **Paul Warchol:** 27, 304, 305, 306.

ORIGINAL ARTWORKS DEPICTED: Parks Anderson: 209 / **Ron Arad:** "2RNot chair," 224–25 / **Dirk Bauer:** "He's Back," 111 / **Mark Bradford:** "The Niña, the Pinta and the Santa Maria," 220–21 / **Edgar Britton:** "Yin and Yang," 274; "Communication," 274; "Aphrodite," 274 / **Dale Chihuly:** 209, 283 / **William Cummings:** 82 / **Martha Daniels:** 274 / **Daum:** Glass Table Lamp, 275 / **Sam Francis:** "Standing Wave," 243, back cover / **Frank Ferrell for Roseville Pottery:** "Moderne Vase," 274; "Russco Vase," 274 / **John Grade:** "Bloom: The Elephant Bed," 56–57 / **Marc Grotjahn:** 224–25 / **Keiko Hara:** 73–74 / **Bernard Hosey:** 76–77, 79 / **William Ingham:** "Red," 209 / **William Ivey:** "Untitled," 1962, 82 / **Anish Kapoor:** "Bracelet," 219 / **Vance Kirkland:** 275 / **Jeff Koons:** "Pluto and Proserpina," 218–19, 222 / **Yayoi Kusama:** "A Tale in Blue Is Filled with My Life," 246–47 / **Fernand Leger:** "Nature Morte," 276 / **Glenn Lignon:** "The Motherland #1," 224–25 / **Linling Lu:** "One Hundred Melodies of Solitude No. 71," 47 / **Richard Luster:** 274 / **Robert Mangold:** "Double Tetrahedralhypershere No. 41," 272, 274 / **Sherry Markovitz:** "Llama," 209, Courtesy of Greg Kucera Gallery / **Joe McDonnell:** "Ice Brigade," 82 / **Robert Motherwell:** "Elegy Study," 70–71 / **Mary Ann Peters:** 284 / **Pablo Picasso:** 209 / **Ricardo Pinto:** "Alignment," 47 / **Jaume Plensa:** "SOUL XII," 197 / **Seth Randal:** "The King," 209; "The Queen," 209 / **Harry Woolliscroft Rhead for Roseville Pottery:** "Mostique Vase," 274; "Mostique Planter," 274 / **Roseville Pottery:** "Futura/Arches Vase," 274; "Futura/Pleated Star Vase," 274; "Futura/The Bomb Vase," 274 / **Richard Royal:** "Relationship Series: Spray," 209 / **Sterling Ruby:** 218–19, Courtesy Sterling Ruby Studio and Gagosian / **Norie Sato:** 209 / **Park Seo-Bo:** "Red Painting," 268 / **Diego Singh:** 240–41 / **Preston Singletary:** 82 / **Julie Spiedel:** 212, Courtesy of Winston Wächter Fine Art / **Lino Tagliapietra:** 80–81 / **Adriana Varejão:** "Monocromo America," 227 / **Edward Wormley for Dunbar Co.:** Low Surfboard Table and Cabinet, 275 / **Frank Lloyd Wright:** Dining Suite and Yellow Peacock Chair, 275 / **Jorge Yazpik:** "Untitled," 46.

On the front cover: Tofino Beach House exterior from the beach (see also pages 236–37); on the back cover: Tofino Beach House living area looking onto the beach, courtesy of Nic Lehoux; pages 2–3: Longbranch Cabin from the beach; pages 4–5: The JW Marriott Los Cabos Beach Resort frames the ocean.

First published in the United Kingdom in 2018 by
Thames & Hudson Ltd, 181A High Holborn, London WC1V 7QX

First published in the United States of America in 2018 by
Thames & Hudson Inc., 500 Fifth Avenue, New York, New York 10110

Reprinted 2024

Jim Olson: Building, Nature, Art © 2018 Thames & Hudson Ltd, London
Introduction text © 2018 Aaron Betsky
Main text, sketches, and architectural plans © 2018 Olson Kundig
For all other images, please see the picture credits list.

Designed by Steve Russell / aka-designaholic.com

British Library Cataloguing-in-Publication Data
A catalogue record for this book is available from the British Library

Library of Congess Control Number 2017958129

ISBN 978-0-500-34333-3

Printed and bound in China by C&C Offset Printing Co. Ltd

Be the first to know about our new releases,
exclusive content and author events by visiting
thamesandhudson.com
thamesandhudsonusa.com
thamesandhudson.com.au

FSC
www.fsc.org
MIX
Paper | Supporting responsible forestry
FSC® C008047